The 20 Minute Sales Coach

Improve Sales Performance & Increase Sales

In As Little As 20 Minutes a Day

Ann-Marie Heidingsfelder

This book is dedicated to all of you busy professionals committed to wild sales success, the success of your customers and living the lives you imagine.

It is also dedicated to my daughter, Anneliese Clare, who is the sunshine of my life and my husband, Robert, who lovingly makes sure I always dot my I's and cross my T's. This book wouldn't be at all possible without their uplifting love and support.

ABOUT THE AUTHOR

Ann Marie Heidingsfelder, sales strategist, executive coach and author, develops engaged, high-impact sales teams and creates outstanding revenue and profitability growth for her corporate clients. Her 25 years of Fortune 100, award winning sales success in technology and healthcare makes her uniquely qualified to guide sales executives in solution selling techniques to increase face to face meetings, deal pipelines and closing ratios. Clients benefit by improved self-management, communication and proven, real world sales strategies. She also coaches executive leadership in competency building and development for improved organizational effectiveness and solid business results.

Ann-Marie holds an MBA, is a certified coach and a member of the Northern California HR Association, Sales Management Association and International Coach Federation. She writes the *Sales Coaching for Success* blog and an advice column that has appeared online at Examiner.com. Her sales articles have also appeared in YFS Magazine, SalesPro Magazine and the Northern California HR Association Magazine.

A native Bostonian, Ann-Marie resides in Sonoma County, CA with her husband, daughter, three cats, dog and a sprawling collection of plants. When she's not coaching or writing you can find her in the garden, on a run, channeling Martha Stewart or managing her daughter's school art docent program. Visit Ann-Marie at partner4successcoaching.com.

Contents

FORWARD

Okay, you've read all the New York Times business best sellers, attended notable sales trainings throughout the years and, frankly, know how to sell. You've been doing it for a while now and have perhaps even experienced significant success and a great income. So how can this little book help you?

Senior sales executives come to coaching for a variety of reasons . . . Perhaps they've lost that "magic" that brought past success, have unidentified current sales process gaps, need to adapt their style to the post-internet sales world (they are still selling like it's 1987 except they no longer have a pager!) or are leaders needing enhanced competency development .
Whatever is coming between you and sales success, this book can help. Spinning your wheels, adapting to changes or just plain falling short of business targets can be very frustrating. This book is for you! It's laid out in bite-sized chapters with information, tips, advice and motivation to get you on track to closing more deals. Perfect for sales professionals who just aren't getting the coaching support they need from management (likely because management either doesn't know how or doesn't have the time). Read a chapter here and there,

follow up with end of chapter goal and planning questions and you'll find you are energized and equipped with new strategies. Who says you can't teach an old dog new tricks? Or remind him of the basics simply forgotten with time?

And if you're in the zippy spring of your career this book is going to provide key strategies to accelerate skill development, improve and reinforce the solution sales process and increase your income.

So if you feel you are working hard without getting the results you need to succeed, discover how to work smarter in the following pages . . .

Happy Selling!

Ann-Marie

HOW TO USE THIS BOOK

"Put your future in good hands — your own."

Mark Victor Hansen

There are very few sales challenges I haven't either personally conquered in my 20+ years as a senior sales executive or helped clients overcome in my sales coaching practice. These sales obstacles are universal. Helping client after client navigate the very same roadblocks to success prompted me to want to write a book to help other account managers - just like you - who are likely experiencing the same.

So whether you are a seasoned account executive that needs a Sales 101 refresher to get back to the fundamentals that initially made you a success or an up and coming sales rep whose enthusiasm still surpasses skill, these pages are for you. The sales coaching for each topic is so brief (but to the point) that, busy as you are, you can read as little as 20 minutes a day to continue working on your sales skill development and competencies.

Using this book is easy. The only required reading is Chapter 1, SMART Goal Setting. Successful coaching depends on concretely identifying the behavior you need to change in order to reach desired business results. That's where the Chapter 1 goal setting and activity plan come in handy! Designed to be a hands-on book, digest any chapter and then quickly and easily create a related sales goal, develop a workable plan and get results fast. It's the same process you'd experience if you were paying several hundred dollars a session for sales coaching! Starting with the goal setting in Chapter 1 provides a base methodology for in making sure targets and plans are achievable and high impact the other chapter topic areas. Otherwise, look up topics in any order and in a quick page or two you are on your way to trying a different method or making a mental shift that is certain to make a difference and increase your sales.

Why is the workbook part of the book valuable? Because sales coaching is not only seeing and understanding new information but Doing it to make new habits stick. *"Plan your work and work your plan"* the saying goes. And what happens if you find that you aren't implementing the changes you want or need to make?

- Find a colleague, manager, sales coach or family member to hold you accountable by sharing your goal and plan

- Re-evaluate the goal

Current research indicates that only about 50% of salespeople achieve quota and 87% of sales training is forgotten within 30 days[1]. While it's acknowledged that sales coaching and sales performance are closely tied, often there is little expertise or time for sales managers to coach where it's needed most in the middle of the performance bell curve. Top sales performers typically don't need sales coaching (more leadership coaching here) for they all share the characteristics of being effective communicators and influencers, resourceful, results-orientated and accountable. So here is your tool to foster those exact top gun success traits despite an absence of management guidance. Congratulations on

---

[1] 1 CSO Insights Sales Performance Optimization Study, March 2010. ; Incentive Insights: How Many Salespeople Should Meet Their Quota, Chad Albrecht, Sales & Marketing Management, July 30, 2010.

taking a step in the right direction and putting your development and sales success in your own hands!

Let's get going!

Write down 3 benefits you want to obtain from reading this book and becoming your own sales performance coach:

1. _____

_____

_____

2. _____

_____

_____

3. _____

_____

_____

SMART GOAL SETTING

"The most important key to achieving great success is to decide upon your goal and launch, get started, take action, move."

John Wooden

Setting Sales Goals You Can Actually Achieve

It's a yearly ritual . . . In offices everywhere sales executives formulate the year's goals and activities needed to reach them. To guarantee that you accomplish your yearly objectives sharpen your success strategy with this checklist:

- ✓ Is your goal specific, measurable and trackable? For example, it's not enough to want to see more new contacts. Get behind that generalization and drill down to what it is you exactly want to accomplish. This prospecting goal instead becomes: "I want to see 2 new prospects per week". Translate your activity into a metric that can be measured and tracked for progress. And s-t-r-e-t-c-h. Make the goal a step beyond what you are currently accomplishing.
- ✓ Is your goal realistic and therefore achievable? If the company average deal size is $250k it very well may be unreasonable to make $500k per deal as your own sales goal.
- ✓ Is your goal well-timed? Milestones and due dates ensure that goals are suitably and sensibly met.

Aim high but make your expectations practical to avoid stress and disappointment. Rome wasn't built in a day so allow a sensible amount of time for getting the job done.

✓ Do you have a genuine commitment to succeed? You may want it, but not badly enough to follow through and do what it takes. Be honest with yourself. Hoping something will happen or be achieved is a far cry from making sure it happens. You'll only make your goal a reality if it's important enough that you wholeheartedly dedicate yourself to its success.

✓ Do you have a clear action plan? You may have a goal and a timeline all right but only a foggy clue – or no idea at all — as to how to make it happen.

"Plan your work and work your plan" we used to say in my first Silicon Valley sales job. Identify the steps you need to take to get where you are going. Without a map who knows where you'll end up! Certainly not where you intended to be. Goal setting can be fun, exciting and invigorating. With commitment, proper planning and implementation you will succeed. You make your own reality . . . So make yours a year dedicated to achieving your sales goals and success!

<u>My Success Plan Template</u>

Tweak this for any specific, measurable goal!

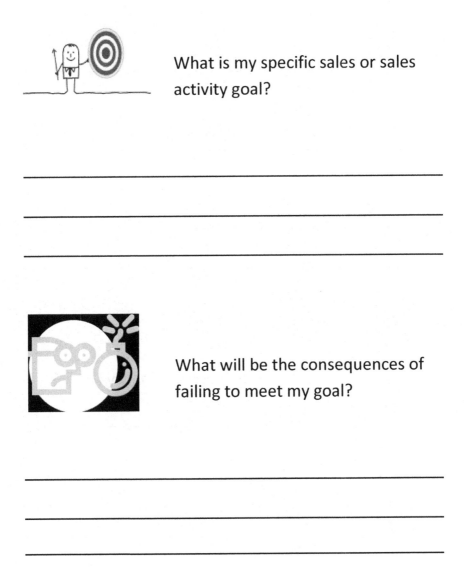

What is my specific sales or sales activity goal?

_____

_____

_____

What will be the consequences of failing to meet my goal?

_____

_____

_____

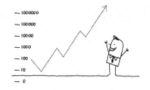

Benefits that come with meeting this goal:

1. _____

   _____

2. _____

   _____

3. _____

   _____

I will achieve my goal by (DATE):

_____

 Resources / people needed to help me:

1. _____

2. _____

3. _____

What would prevent me from achieving my goal?

1. _____

_____

2. _____

_____

3. _____

_____

Methods for getting back on track
should I lose focus:

1. _____

_____

2. _____

_____

3. _____

_____

NETWORK YOUR WAY TO SUCCESS

It's not what you know but who you know that makes the difference.

Anonymous

Get More Leads From Networking Groups

Every top salesperson agrees that networking is a key activity to obtaining more and quality prospects. If you attend events aimlessly roaming around sucking down cocktails and free munchies convinced that you are "networking", you are totally missing out. Here are a few things to remember to get the most out of the groups that you join:

- **Give more than you take.** Find opportunities to learn about the business and personal interests of the other members with an aim to help them out with information and leads. Ask curious questions. And contrary to popular wisdom, don't be so quick to spew your elevator pitch. People love to talk about themselves – not you. These contact centered interactions are more likely to form a firm foundation for long-term relationships. Be sure to follow up with a quick note or LinkedIn invitation.

- **Volunteer on committees or offer to be a guest speaker.** In helping others you will find that you build credibility and visibility that's sure to keep you top of mind and translate into leads.

- **Attend learning sessions.** Professional and industry groups offer webinars and seminars to educate members on trends and focus topics. Being a trusted advisor to your customers requires that you stay on top of industry developments anyhow. While at GE Healthcare Financial Services I joined the Healthcare Financial Management Association and attended conferences targeted at my prospect base of hospital CFOs. Not only were these great networking opportunities, but I learned much about what was keeping my clients up at night. So while my competitors were asking this over-used question directly, I was able to come to customer meetings already prepared with solutions.

- **Choose groups that are fun!** If you're not having fun in your group, you should be doing something else. Enjoy socializing while you also increase both friendships and your profile. There are groups like the Executive Women's Golf Association that are completely based on fun and engaging interests. So why not get some rest and relaxation in while you are building up your contact base?

Networking groups can be a fabulous source of increased sales. According to one business owner of a sound and video production company, a whopping 70% of his business comes from his San Jose Chamber of Commerce contacts and volunteering as Ambassador for its new members. Like any activity, you'll get out what you put into it.

My Networking Success Plan

What is my networking goal?

_____

_____

_____

_____

 Benefits that come with meeting this goal:

1. _____

2. _____

3. _____

Three professional or networking organizations I want to join and 3 benefits of membership:

1. _____

_____

2. _____

_____

3. _____

_____

Milestones & Dates:

_____

_____

What would prevent me from achieving my goal?

1. _____

2. _____

3. _____

 Methods for getting back on track
should I lose focus:

1. _____

_____

2. _____

_____

3. _____

_____

LinkedIn: Networking Your Way to Sales Success

If you aren't using LinkedIn for prospecting and staying in front of your customers you are missing a great sales opportunity. LinkedIn is the go-to social network for professionals and touts a whopping 313 million worldwide subscribers (as of the time of this publication). Business- focused, it's the perfect vehicle to publicly highlight your skills, services, company and insights as a thought leader. It provides yet another touch point for clients and prospects and helps keep you top of mind by providing a venue for posting valuable updates, articles, whitepapers and the like. Use the "Follow" option to stay abreast of target companies and you're on your way to staying informed of developments that can help you connect with prospects on a deeper level.

Here's a LinkedIn success checklist:

- ✓ Add your LinkedIn address to your email signature with an invitation, "**Connect with me on LinkedIn: [YOUR URL]**"

- ✓ Reach out by phone and email to let others know you are sending them an invite. Don't connect with people you don't know! Establish a connection through a shared contact, one of the many LinkedIn groups or an affiliation (like your alma mater or former employer). Be sure to personalize your invitation. There's nothing worse than receiving LinkedIn's canned template.
- ✓ Join and participate in groups by identifying ones to which your contacts and target market belong (50 is currently the maximum allowed). Join industry groups to stay abreast of developments and trends.
- ✓ Post regular updates to your contacts and groups including wins highlighting your projects and accomplishments.
- ✓ Start and participate in group discussions for increased visibility and to become established as a thought leader.
- ✓ Send a personal thank you note to those who connect or view your profile

Also check your Profile:

- ✓ Adjust your settings and set to public viewing.

✓ Use a professional or interesting photo.

✓ Make your title descriptive. Top networking gurus agree that your headline is one of the most valuable sections of real estate on your profile. It should be worded to give readers an idea of what you can do for them, or to promote your experience and expertise. For example, if you provide accounting services to small businesses you can improve your header by saying *"QuickBooks™ Expert"*.

✓ Keep your profile current with new experiences, projects and business- related recommended reading. Send these updates to all your connections using the Share feature.

✓ Your Summary section should tell not only what you do but what you value professionally. Tie in personal details whenever possible. One of my contacts who is a power user and sales recruiter writes about his passion for biking and draws business excellence analogies using his athletic feats which makes for a riveting summary of his recruiting business.

✓ Get Recommendations from clients, managers and associates to support your skills and experience. Use LinkedIn's automatic profile assessment feature to make sure your profile is complete.

✓ Like any website password make your LinkedIn one unique for your protection.

My LinkedIn Success Plan

What are my goals in using LinkedIn?

1. _____

_____

2. _____

_____

3. _____

_____

How will achieving my goals affecting my sales?

_____

_____

_____

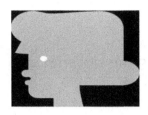

Top three LinkedIn profile areas I need to improve:

1. _____

2. _____

3. _____

What would stop me from engaging consistently on LinkedIn?

_____

_____

_____

_____

_____

 How will I stay active on the LinkedIn site and in its groups?

1. _____

_____

2. _____

_____

3. _____

_____

REACH KEY DECISION MAKERS & BUILD PIPELINE

Sales just don't fall from the sky like manna from heaven. Make a plan for reaching the right people and creating more opportunity!

Dread Cold Calling?

The good news is that you're not alone. Most salespeople find cold calling a dreary and daunting task. However, with an attitude adjustment and planning you can cold call your way to more face to face meetings and increase sales. Consider:

- **What's the worst thing that will happen if you don't prospect?** The answer isn't a good one — is it? Now, think thorough all the benefits resulting from cold call success. Keep your list of positive results in front of you while on the phone to keep you motivated.

- **Avoid the procrastination bug** by scheduling "sacred" cold calling time into your week. Have set time blocks free from all distraction to ensure the task gets completed. That means allowing incoming calls to roll into voicemail, giving email a rest and politely telling cubicle intruders you are working on a project and will get back to them when completed.

- **Reward yourself when your "shift" is done** with a break that includes something fun or relaxing.

Eventually, you'll find the results obtained are reward enough.

- **Use a hard line in a quiet place.** There's nothing more irritating to us all than an unsolicited caller fading in and out on their cell phone.

- **Get referred whenever possible.** Prospects are always more apt to take your call when there's a mutual acquaintance to provide an introduction. Brainstorm all your sources including co-workers, partners, complimentary vendors, LinkedIn contacts and people in your social circles.

  When you can't get referred and need contact names, on-line people finder services such as zoominfo.com can help you identify prospects by various means including company and title. My clients have used these with great success.

- **Research your contact and his company.** Doing your homework builds trust and credibility and shows just how important you consider the prospect and his business.

- **Build confidence and rely on a script or talking points.** This helps avoid

  "Um" and hesitation as you have only a single shot to make a great first impression.

- **Be absolutely convinced in your own mind** that the prospect wants to hear what you have to say. A positive outlook produces sureness in your voice that helps secure your listener's attention. Don't be too cute or chatty but do be relaxed.

- **In a single sentence state your purpose** – the benefit or value you propose. What's in it for the prospect to take your call?

- **Timing is everything.** Be certain your contact is ready to hear what you have to say. *"I appreciate your busy schedule, Mr. X. Is this a convenient time to speak for 15 minutes?* If not follow up with *"When might be a better time to schedule a call with you?"* It's truly annoying to have a cold caller jump breathlessly into a spiel while one desperately tries to interject that he or she is in the middle of a project or meeting.

- **Anticipate objections** as they are certain to come your way. The best defense is to be prepared with

a compelling offer. Highlight the insight or value
your prospect stands to gain by speaking with you.

And remember . . . Cold calling success is always based
on client pain and its impact. It isn't an opportunity for a
product "feature dump".

Cold calling needn't be fearful or an energy drain if you
are prepared. And remember that it's a numbers game.
The more calls made, the more *"yes"* responses
received!

My Cold Calling Success Plan

What's my weekly cold calling goal?

_____

_____

What will happpen if I don't cold call?

_____

_____

I will schedule "sacred" cold calling time every week (DAYS/TIMES)?

_____

_____

Three ways cold calling will contribute to my sales success:

1. _____

2. _____

3. _____

Resources / people I need to help me:

1. _____

_____

2. _____

_____

3. _____

_____

What would prevent me from achieving my goal?

1. _____

_____

2. _____

_____

3. _____

_____

 Methods for getting staying on track:

1. _____

_____

2. _____

_____

3. _____

_____

Focus On the High Probability Deals

Back in my early selling days one of my peers was this incredibly driven young guy who was constantly bringing in unsuitable deals. He provided much entertainment at sales meetings where we account managers would chuckle as he seriously described potential deals that clearly sounded like he was working for another company — or in a completely different industry. This misguided sales rep was regularly trying to fit the round peg in the square hole of our financing solutions to the chagrin of management, himself and that of his prospects. It didn't win him any internal supporters and it cost him sales. Management would see this rep coming down the hall and walk the other way knowing that he was going browbeat them for deal approval that was clearly outside the organization's realm. I can only imagine that his customers understood he was full of promises that couldn't be kept.

Knowing your company's "sweet spot" helps you identify opportunities that you actually can win. Fish or cut bait by letting go of or delegating for routine support the ones that are outside your company's abilities. It seems counterintuitive to some salespeople who naturally want to win them all. The truth is you can't. Thoroughly understanding what deals your company wants to execute and matching this with the right prospects is a winning strategy. Don't waste precious selling time trying to create a solution based on hope versus reality. Prospects and clients alike will appreciate your honesty and integrity in advising how you can realistically help them. The trust that you have their best interests at heart is certain to benefit you in the future when the likelihood for a better match may surface. Realizing where you stand in the industry and what your organization does and does not do well will help you identify and close more deals — and gain management support when you need it most.

On the flip side there are those companies that really do try to be all things to all people. Managers themselves will twist into pretzels to accommodate out of the box solutions. But if your company can't implement them well it could spell disaster. As a sales professional your reputation is paramount. It's the one thing you take from employer to employer throughout your career. So if management is pushing you to sell a solution you clearly have no confidence in - push back. Otherwise, document with management the process, potential pitfalls and checks and balances that will be used to support both you and the customer so you don't find yourself dangling out on a limb without a net during implementation or after delivery.

Finally, a word about RFPs . . . Generally unless you have been involved very early in the customer's solution and buying process you are being used as fodder in an obligatory bidding exercise. These exercises are best left to your support staff unless you truly want to get in deep and do an end run around your competitor. There are very specific strategies for this. Otherwise . . .

Determine what types of high-probability-to-close deals you should spend time on below:

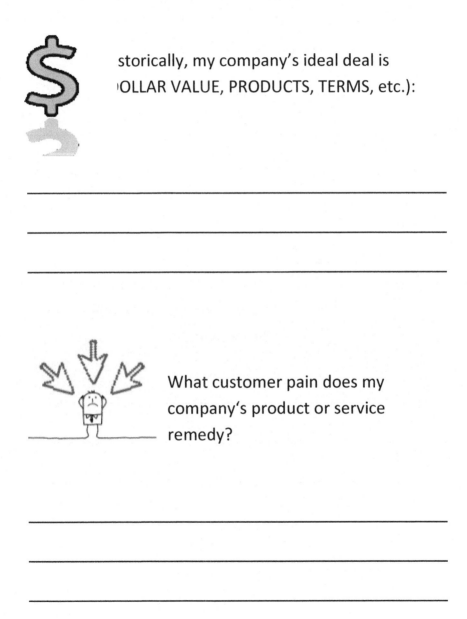

storically, my company's ideal deal is
ꞮOLLAR VALUE, PRODUCTS, TERMS, etc.):

_____

_____

_____

What customer pain does my
company's product or service
remedy?

_____

_____

_____

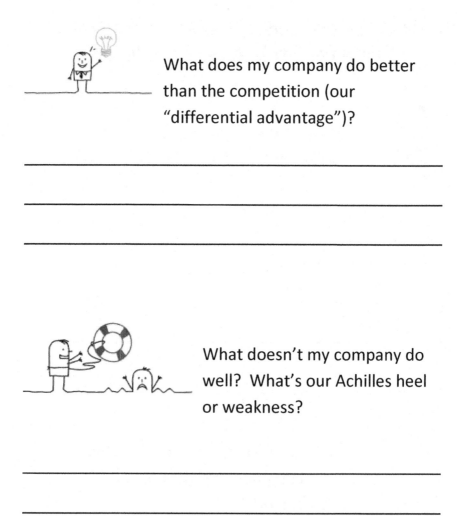

What does my company do better than the competition (our "differential advantage")?

_____

_____

_____

What doesn't my company do well? What's our Achilles heel or weakness?

_____

_____

_____

How well does my company implement customer requests that fall outside of our normal offering?

_____

_____

_____

_____

_____

Don't Waste Time on the Wrong Prospects

Sadly, I encounter many service professionals who spread their market efforts out over a virtual ocean of opportunities. These are people who blindly throw precious time and resources willy nilly in an effort to gain clients . . . Never really knowing or understanding that the secret to success is carving out a very specific niche. Creating differential value for a specific set of clients based on industry knowledge, insights and organizational needs is key to target marketing.

You may have a best-in-class business offering but are truly dead in the water if you don't target people who are the most motivated to purchase from you. You may think that everyone in the Northern Hemisphere is a potential lead, but ask yourself who would make the very Best customer. The model client wants what you have, when you have it and to satisfy some specific need or problem. If you haven't identified your ideal prospect now is the time to do it. It's critical to effectively channeling your marketing efforts, dollars and time for the greatest impact. Identifying your ideal customer leads you to uncover what they read, the organizations they join, other products they buy and where they frequent. Understanding your target market, the motivations of its members and where to find them is paramount to successful lead generation.

An example is selling real estate. There are specialties including entry level, luxury, vacation homes and condos. Within each of these categories one can penetrate even further. The entry level home category consists of buyers who are first time owners, women, and investors among others. Comprising the first time owner category are young families, technology sector employees, singles — again among others. Delve even further into young families and one can classify a certain geography, income level and interests. Are you seeing the picture? The more you drill down to a very specific ideal client the better your chances at successfully targeting this niche.

But what about all those other oh so alluring prospects? The pie has many slices, but you simply can't eat them all. Carving out a specialty allows you to get to know your buyer and develop vertical expertise. Buyers gravitate towards sellers who speak their language and truly understand their unique needs. Write down the details of your perfect client. What do they look like?

How old? Where do they live? What do they do? What other services do they purchase? Keep asking questions until you can create a very specific target profile. Research their hot buttons and become the go-to expert at addressing their particular requirements. Everyone feels more comfortable in the hands of a trusted professional who absolutely understands their world.

Determining your best customer is just the first step — albeit a major one — in selling for results. Trying to be all things to all people can leave you with a jack-of-all-trades reputation and undermine your credibility. So mine those prospects . . . Toss the stones and search out the gold nuggets. You may not give as many presentations or have as many meetings but the ones you do nail will be more likely to have their interest piqued.

Consider the following to make sure you target the right prospects:

Describe the profile of your ideal client – including specific role, industry, title, etc.

_____

_____

_____

_____

_____

_____

What problems do they have that I can solve?

1. _____

2. _____

3. _____

Three places I can find these prospects online or in person:

1. _____

2. _____

3. _____

Steps I need to take to engage my ideal client in these places:

1. _____

_____

2. _____

_____

3. _____

_____

How to Keep Your Pipeline Full

David, a talented account executive with several years of experience, spent the second half of last year totally focused on a $1MM+ technology sale sure to nail his yearly quota. It was truly a make or break situation. And it didn't come out to his advantage. At the 11th hour the deal unexpectedly went south, leaving David demoralized and way below his yearly sales target. To make matters worse, he spent the first half of the new year in rebuilding mode with no idea where his new business would come from.

Don't let this happen to you. Large deals can surely put you over the top — boosting both your sales career and pocketbook. But be careful putting all your sales eggs into one large basket.

The solution is to "make more noise". That is, be certain that you create a robust pipeline of deals of all sizes to ensure making your quota. Relying on a single account or large deal is like playing roulette. One never knows what bullet may get shot at the very last minute leaving you with no back up to fill in a very wide gap in sales.

Determine with your manager's help how much you should have in the pipeline given the length of your sales cycle, average deal size and closing ratios. Dedicate scared prospecting time on your calendar cultivate meet more prospects and create more opportunities – balancing this with closing the deals on which you may be already working. A good start is determining how many face to face meetings you need to add a single deal to the funnel and create a success plan (page 15) to get these booked. When you religiously execute on the prospecting activities you should do every week (cold calling, follow ups, emails, meetings, etc.), your pipeline, quota and commissions will all take care of themselves.

So make certain that you aren't abandoning prospecting just because there's a large, hopeful transaction pending. Prospecting never takes a rest. If you need support, ask for it. At the end of the day you are accountable for a sales goal so identify and obtain the assistance required to square smaller deals with the bigger, time-consuming opportunities. The road to success in sales is one in which you need not only a high revving performance engine but also plenty of quality gas to prevent stalls and get you to your final destination on time!

Fill in the blanks to discover what your ideal pipeline value should be and how many weekly customer meetings are needed to get there.

My pipeline needs to be [HOW MANY TIMES] _____ my sales quota which is [DOLLARS] $_____.

This translates to [DOLLAR VALUE] $_____ of REAL* deals pending. (*These are deals that are past the stage where you are still trying to stimulate prospect interest.)

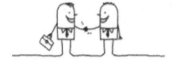

To accomplish this I need [NUMBER] _____ customer/prospect meetings per week.

Of these, [NUMBER] _____ need to be new contacts.

What can get in my way of on-going pipeline development?

1. _____

    _____

2. _____

    _____

3. _____

    _____

Methods for staying on track with pipeline development:

1. _____

    _____

2. _____

_____

3. _____

_____

More on Sowing Seeds While Harvesting Year End Deals

It's natural for salespeople to be completely obsessed with the A1 priority of pulling in contracts and orders prior to fiscal year end. In fact, it's career limiting not to make your number. Even so, salespeople need to balance this with critical business development – creating more opportunities – to keep sales pipelines full going into the next year. But while you're busy picking what remains of this year's harvest how do you also prepare for next year's crop? Most complex B2B transactions have long selling cycles. So if you're not sowing seeds today it's likely you're going to hit what could be a potentially protracted lull in future quarters.

To compound matters, it may be hard to get the attention of potential customers especially at fiscal year-end. They're likely managing the same deadlines you are – closing the books, reeling in projects, making next year's budget and personnel decisions as well as meeting their own revenue targets.

So what's an account manager to do? Make the time to look hard at your annual goals and plan, plan, plan.

Scope out legitimate deals that will get you off to a fast start in the early months of your new fiscal year. Now back into these deals by creating actionable items that you can work on TODAY. Your clients should be looking to you as the industry expert (if not, that's a whole other chapter!). So confidently coach your prospects to be proactive in Q4 for ordering in Q1 & Q2:

- **Plan internal opportunity reviews** to gather input from your managers and other stakeholders on your team. Together scope out challenges and options as well as brainstorm and formulate your strategies for the new fiscal year deals.

- **Create a sense of urgency for prospects** to plan more sooner than later. Create impetus with solid *"why now"* motives for mapping out next year's deals now.

- **Offer to partner on the client's heavy** lifting (action requests) as an incentive for them to provide you with time for planning as well as access to key influencers and decision makers within the account.

- **Co-create with customers project timelines and milestones.** Collaborate on concrete action items that will keep them on track to move future projects and deals along. Distribute the results to all stakeholders internal and external to help raise the visibility and keep everyone on track both this quarter and into the new year.

- **Get verbal agreements on everything** you and the client jointly map out and provide a written (email) summary to all parties. Resending the email provides a gentle reminder of their agreements should the deal start going sideways.

Sales is a rewarding and challenging career. However, you're only as good as your last month, quarter or year. So be sure to sink those deals in front of you begging for attention — while keeping a keen eye on the horizon as next year will be here before you know it!

Q4 Success Plan to Keeping Pipeline Deals Moving& Growing

 Three (3) things I can do to tee up next quarter's orders while closing my end of year deals:

1. _____

   _____

2. _____

   _____

3. _____

   _____

What's the result of failing to add to next year's pipeline?

_____

_____

_____

 What are the benefits?

1. _____

   _____

2. _____

   _____

3. _____

   _____

Steps I need to promote next quarter or year's deals now:

1. _____

   _____

2. _____

   _____

3. _____

   _____

People or resources I need to help me:

1. _____

   _____

2. _____

   _____

3. _____

   _____

 What will I do to stay on track?

_____

_____

_____

How to Win In a Down Economy

How do you create more interest in your product or service and increase sales and revenue in uncertain economic times? Perhaps individuals and companies in your industry aren't purchasing as much or at all right now. Many firms are reserving cash so they can nimbly react to changing circumstances. For others revenues may be down or expenses up. For still others who have critical needs, there may be delays due to lack of confidence. What's a sales person to do?

Now more than ever, it's imperative to focus, not on transactions, but relationships. Relationships have always been the foundation of solid, repeat business and referrals. Today's environment has reaffirmed that importance. So don't "sell"– engage. Engaging prospects is a process of attraction and creating rapport and trust. Once attracted, hold their attention and participate in their business strategies. But how?

- **Build relationships by being curious.** Do your homework with thorough research. Ask high impact questions of your prospects to fully grasp their challenges, business and vision as well as demonstrate your own understanding.

- **Hone listening skills** to clearly hear their pain points and overall goals. Get behind their mere words to understand what they are really saying.

- **Query with "How can I help you *right now*?"**

- **Become an expert and a reliable resource** in your industry to create added value.

- **Maintain constant contact.** Develop a regular call and meeting schedule to stay abreast of your prospect's changing needs and sense of urgency. Don't write a customer off because they aren't buying today. If you're somewhat sure of a latent need be persistent. Remaining top of mind and keeping them on your own radar screen is sure to get you an opportunity when the situation changes.

- **Expand your network to include other partners or vendors** who sell into the same space and whose products complement your own. Synergy with third parties may help drive sales where your standalone products can't - offering clients a more total solution. Credibility also grows with first-

71

hand knowledge of your prospect's related projects and how yours ties in.

- **Sweep the corners in prospecting.** Expand your reach beyond obvious decision makers in target companies and include potential influencers, allies and end-users to your roster of contacts. Multiple contacts over various functional areas give valuable insights into the dynamics of an organization. They often serve as a reality check for what the decision maker is telling (or not telling) you. Allies are friendly contacts who enjoy providing information and coaching to help better position you and your product with key decision makers. Be honest and genuine in these friendships. It's obvious and distasteful to others when one is being opportunistic. So seek to find others with whom you can connect on a more personal level and who would like to help you succeed.

Customer hesitation demands thinking beyond the individual sale. Building relationships takes the stress out of selling and actually makes your job more enjoyable. You'll win supporters, enhance your reputation and find yourself in the strong position of influencer. Appreciate the process knowing that it's not "if" but "when" a sales opportunity arrives.

 Three (3) of my accounts that aren't ready to buy due to economic or other factors:

1. _____

_____

2. _____

_____

3. _____

_____

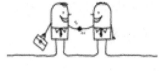 Three (3) things I can do in these accounts to build better long-term relationships:

1. _____

_____

2. _____

_____

3. _____

_____

Draw a company organization chart and find where you have holes. Use the goals template on page 15 to make a concrete plan to meet these people!

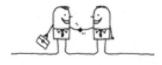 What potential selling partners are in the account?

1. _____

_____

2. _____

_____

3. _____

_____

I will contact them by [DATE] _____ to arrange a networking meeting:

What is my timeline for regular account contact?

_____

_____

BETTER COMMUNICATON =
BETTER RESULTS

"Seek first to understand, then to be understood."

Steven Covey

For High Impact Customer Meetings, Less Is More

"Silence Is a Source of Great Strength"

Lao Tzu

I remember my first outside sales position for public employee retirement plans back in the '80s (before some of you were born – ouch!). I was lucky enough to have great rapport with the area VP two levels above me and so he offered one day to accompany me on sales calls. We had a couple of introductory meetings before we found ourselves in yet another grade school classroom with a teacher to whom I was making my long-winded pitch. There were just so many great benefits of our retirement savings plan and I must tell them all! In addition, VP Jay was sure to be impressed with how well I knew the product features so early in my tenure. Needless to say, the call dead-ended like a Back Bay alley just like the previous ones of the day — with the prospect "thinking about it".

Once back in the car, Jay looked at me and calmly said, "You talk too much". Not good news for anyone who knows me and how much I love to talk. It was the most valuable feedback I have ever received. I made a vow that day to hone my listening skills. Shortly thereafter I made President's Club.

As a senior account manager I went on to mentor many salespeople, who as we say in the business, "threw up" all over customers – messily spewing product features at these confused victims. It's assumed that if you throw enough mud at a wall some of it is bound to stick! Like me on that day with Jay, whether from nervousness or a genuine lack of solution selling expertise, these reps never get the sale. Truth is, few people are comfortable with silence — especially highly social sales people. The tendency when one hears a void in conversation is to fill it. It takes a strong, confident salesperson to know when to sit back, simply shut up and give the customer time to think or do the talking.

What's the solution? Remember that sales calls are not about demonstrating the breadth of your product knowledge. So leave the 60 slide PowerPoint at the office. It's not even about you or your product per se. . . . It's about the customer and where he is in the buying cycle. What he needs and what he thinks. Ask high-impact, open-ended questions and L-I-S-T-E- N actively. Be comfortable asking and, yes, being silent for as long as it takes your customer to reflect and answer. Practice with your family and friends. When you feel the urge to jump in with an answer or further information listen some more. With repetition and success, like me, listening that comes from silence will be one of your greatest selling strengths!

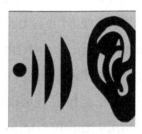

Assess your listening skills!

What distracts me from listening at times?

_____

Do I let the customer finish talking before I jump in?

_____

Am I thinking about what I am going to say next while my customer is talking?

_____

Do I pay attention to non-verbal cues?

_____

Do I come prepared to my meetings with several high impact questions?

_____

Do I get behind the mere words of what the customer is saying to get to the real meaning? Asking a question behind their question for clarity?

_____

Do I assume too much without getting clarification?

_____

Do I summarize and repeat back what the customer has said to make sure I have understood?

_____

Do I fully understand my company's solution (not features!)?

_____

Why Being Liked Won't Get You the Sale

I recently had a sales manager refer one of his reps to me for coaching to "up" her customer conversations. Seems this seasoned AE had plenty of existing relationships in her sole account but was running out of compelling reasons for meetings and the client discussions she did have weren't resulting in new opportunities. Fact is, this sales rep, (let's call her Nancy) liked to talk about pretty much everything except business. She'd discuss all range of personal topics like her dogs, plane trips and kids in college. Anything but business. As she told me, she knew her contacts for years and was a true "relationship rep".

Regrettably for Nancy, companies don't hire reps because their customers need more friends. Nor do C-level decision makers want to take precious time out of a busy day for AEs to drop in and *see how it's going*. According to Harvard Business Review, the highest performing sales people are experts, closers and consultants. Socializers fall into the bucket called "the rest" and make up about 15% of reps. A socializer is someone who may hit it off with customers at first by putting them at ease with idle chit-chat. But sadly, these reps never bring valuable insights to their customers and prospects to build vision, get pain acknowledged and position their solutions for creating opportunity – let alone close a deal.

Customers expect salespeople to stimulate the sales process, to ask the right questions and finally to *ask for their business*. When this initiative or confidence is lacking, no matter how much they like you personally, they aren't going to respect or value you as a business partner. I have seen customers actually relieved by a change in account management when they were subjected to a salesperson that was so very nice but brought so little value.

How do you know if you are talking too much about all the wrong things? Management observation and feedback, measurement and assessments are helpful. In Nancy's case, her sales manager witnessed first-hand her tendency to banter which was backed up by a very anemic pipeline. In addition, communications assessments for salespeople are full of insight into what one's natural style is and how well they adapt that style to the demands of the job. Truth is, it's okay to be a natural socializer as long as you adjust your style in order to reach your sales goals.

__Discover how to get your FREE communications assessment!__

__See the Selling Tools and Resources in the Appendix__

Compelling Emails Guarantee Replies

Many of my coaching clients, including very well-seasoned senior sales professionals, are stumped as how to get their sales-related email read. How does one compose a compelling sales email that prompts a reply - especially to a meeting request or a status on a pending order? Way back when Sales 101 taught us all **KISS** ("Keep It Simple Stupid!") – yet many client emails I edit are longer than Moby Dick. Fact is, we are all drowning under a tsunami of Inbox arrivals. So if your email doesn't stand out and grab the reader it will likely be relegated to the wasteland of the unread or worse – the deleted items folder – without so much as glance. According to email marketers, open rates continue to be on the decline due to the increasingly large volume readers receive. To increase your chances of sales email success:

- **Keep the header to 40 characters or less** and use compelling words. My assistant recently sent me an email titled "Important Question". Guess which one I opened first?

- **Use a salutation.** It's amazing the number of sales emails I see that aren't personalized and so look like spam.

- **Focus on a single, clear message.** What's your objective? To get a meeting, a status, etc.?

- **Use the customer's perspective, not your own.** Avoid the use of the words "I" and "We". Talk in terms of what's in it for the reader to reply – their benefit, not yours. Sadly, nobody cares what you want . . . as in "I would like to meet with you."

- **Keep your email message brief.** Save the lengthy reference stories and details for a meeting.

- **Keep the email visually clean and easy to scan** by using bullets and bolding key ideas in the text in a way that makes sense.

- **Avoid marketing puffery**, i.e. *"We're the market leader with the best solutions on earth"* as well as laundry listing your product's features.

- **Don't end by asking permission** as in *"Can I call you?"* Assume they want to talk! Give your reader a couple of options from which to choose for following up.

- **Create an email signature** that markets your company – including logo, website and tagline.

- **Test your results and adjust accordingly.** Try several variations of an email solicitation and see which one produces the best results for your industry.

Here's an example of a follow up email I actually sent to a client who wasn't responding to a submitted proposal (I received an immediate reply!). It's short, direct and has a strong call to action.

Subject Header: Please reply: Still interested in sales coaching?

Email Body:

Good Morning Sanjay:

Well, you're fast approaching your April 1st. need date . . . Please be so kind as to share where you are in the selection process for the training and coaching.

What day and time next week are you available for a follow up call?

Thank you very much for your continued consideration. Have yourself a fabulous weekend!

Email Signature:

Warmly,

Ann-Marie

Ann-Marie Heidingsfelder,
Sales Performance & Leadership Coach

Partner4Success

TEL: 707-526-6911

Have you visited our website lately? Check out the latest resources to help you increase customer meetings, pipeline & sales:

partner4successcoaching.com *

*Variations of my signature include links to LinkedIn, Twitter and Facebook as well as any coaching promotions I may have going on.

Get To the Point

"Some people have a way with words, and other people...oh, uh, not have way."

Steve Martin

Customers scratching their heads in confusion over why you've contacted them aren't in need of yet another lost-in-the woods sales presentation. Instead of dazing them with directionless conversation give them a compass — clear, concise language that drives your points home. Direct, confident language can convey your ideas and value with conviction. This means the difference between a persuasive point that brings in the order and one that limply falls flat. Great communication is manna for reaching your sales goals. Instead of dragging down dialogue with weak, ineffective expressions use positive, straightforward wording to create credibility and spur your customer to action.

Radiate confidence in your next customer exchange by speaking or writing with assertiveness. The following feeble words are better talking wishes with your fairy godmother. Instead, use their more powerful replacements at right.

- Should, Probably, Could, Would → Will

- Hope → Expect

- If → When

Avoid bland as white toast words and phrases such as:

- I think/believe/feel/wonder

- Hopefully

- It seems

- Fairly

- Would it be okay (if) . . .

Imagine the difference in customer response to the following examples.

"I think this widget is what you need to double production" and *"This widget is what you need to double production"*.

"I hope you're available Thursday to meet" and *"When are you available Thursday to meet?"*

And unless you're vendor to the Miley Cyrus-inspired set you'll want to toss meaningless qualifiers like the below:

- So, like . . ., right?

- Sort of / kind of

- Um

- You know

Qualifying sentence starters also weaken your message: Stay away from the likes of *"In all honesty . . ."* , *"Truthfully . . ."* and *"Basically . . ."* as well as trite, overused phrases such as *"At the end of the day . . ."* and *"Thank you for your time".* You can be <u>much</u> more specific with the last one here (thank them for what specifically?).

Avoid using acronyms, overly technical or company-specific terms your listener won't understand.

These types of expressions dilute the point you are trying to make. Deleting them keeps your sentences crisp, assured and content rich — making sure your idea doesn't get lost in a bunch of linguistic mumbo jumbo.

Weak language also creates an unrefined image. Avoid unprofessional slang like *"yeah"* and *"nah"* that makes you sound like a teenager. The words are actually *"yes"* and *"no"*.

As top leadership trainers attest, using words like *"sort of"*, *"maybe" and "should"* all cast distrust in our prospects minds. More convincing words let prospects know that our offering is right for them, we're certain our solution works, and it adds to our credibility when we demonstrate passion about our products. Using compelling words helps get our prospects thinking, *"Yes this will solve my problem!"*

People buy on emotion versus logic. Using words to help demonstrate to our clients how our service benefits them, clearly, succinctly with affirmative language gets our client motivated about our offer. As a result our prospects turn into clients more quickly.

Remember that you can drive up in a Maserati, be wearing Prada and represent the latest and greatest new technology but if communication fails you, you're punting. Practice what the sales pros know – that to be a winner you need to consistently choose high impact speech that influences outcomes.

What's something you do you when speaking that is excessive or unnecessary?

Ask family, friends and colleagues or even record yourself. You may be speaking ineffectively without even realizing it!

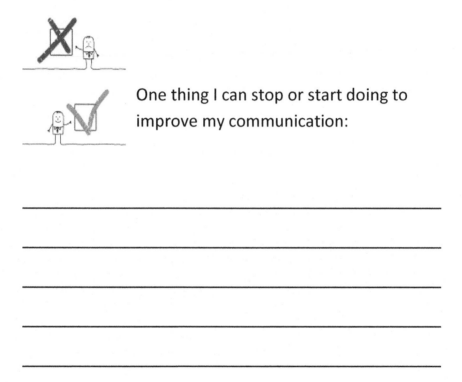

One thing I can stop or start doing to improve my communication:

_____

_____

_____

_____

_____

How will this change benefit me and my customers?

_____

_____

_____

_____

_____

Handwritten Notes Say More Than *"Thanks"*

There is nothing more impressive or personal than a handwritten note. It suggests a politeness that is greatly lacking in the flood of digital communicating today. And it truly fosters greater civility in today's etiquette vacuum. A note scripted in your own hand is especially required whenever you need to express thanks or appreciation. It tells the recipient that they are important — that you took precious time out of a busy day just for them. Sales meetings, new or recent orders, pertinent information and referrals all qualify for this personal way of showing gratitude.

- Use the best quality notecards with your and the company information imprinted on them. Both stationary and content should impress the reader.

- "Dear" or the more casual "Hello" is an appropriate salutation which is then followed by brief sentences of sincere thanks.

- Add a sentence or two about the benefit of the transaction or the value of the relationship to you both.

- There are several closes depending on how formal you wish your communication to be. "(Warm) regards" or "Best" is customary. Omitting a closing and writing only your name at the end is proper as well. Always save "Love" for close family and personal friends only. It is never used in business correspondence.

Handwritten notes are an ideal method to strengthen your business relationships and forge new ones. They are more memorable and intimate that than an email – which, by the way, is okay to send if time is constrained. Proper etiquette dictates that your appreciation be timely - handwritten or not (mailed within 24 hours of the trigger event). Your thoughtful communication will highlight how highly you value your customers and business associates. Successful salespeople know that strong, valued relationships are critical to driving business success.

And don't stop with thank you notes. Keep up more personal communication throughout the year with birthday and greeting cards and hand written notes for any occasion.

Three (3) things I can do to personalize my communication:

1. _____

2. _____

3. _____

Steps I need to take to make sure this gets done:

1. _____

2. _____

3. _____

What are the benefit(s) for me and my customers?

_____

_____

Managing Up: Better Communicate With Your Boss

Don't assume your boss is a communications expert. Communication skills many times don't come naturally nor are they taught. In addition, many managers are too busy putting out fires and keeping senior managers satisfied — to the point where you may get little direction as to how to do your job effectively. So stop knocking your head against a wall trying to figure out what your manager wants, when and why.

To be successful and advance your sales career consider the following:

- **Understand expectations.** Don't presume to know what your manager requires. Not sure you thoroughly understand sales performance metrics and management objectives? Directly ask for clarification when in doubt. Follow up by documenting the requirements in an email that you can then use as back up for future discussion.

- **Once you understand the objectives, get clear agreement on plans and timelines.** I had a client who, as new rep, developed a sales plan to exclusively sell over the phone. Management's sales plan included 3 days a week in face to face meetings. When this client didn't meet his yearly quota he was put on a performance improvement plan and sent to me for coaching! Agreeing up front on the right customer engagement strategy would have saved time, money and frustration — and increased sales sooner.

- **Ask for support.** It's not a sign of weakness but of resourcefulness. Before approaching your manager, however, have all your ducks in a row: thoroughly analyze the issue, exhaust all options available to you, be clear about your goal and make sure it's within your manager's realm to provide the support you seek. Managers loathe complainers. Be solutions-orientated in your approach or be perfectly honest that you are stumped.

- **Request regular progress meetings.** Don't wait until the tail end of a sale to update your manager that it's going south. Or until your performance review to find that you're not meeting requirements. Instead of waiting for your manager to check –in offer to provide regular updates. No time to meet? Emails or status memos ensure everyone is literally on the same page.

- **Be a team player.** Get on board with what the organization wants to achieve. Tie in how your work and proposed solutions help meet the overall objectives. You'll drown trying to swim against a strong current. Being known as a team player increases your credibility and management's trust – leading to more empowerment and influence.

- **If your manager hasn't taken an interest in your career development, take the initiative** and compose talking points for your next review that include your short and long term career goals. Get buy-in and co-create a development plan with regular progress checks.

Your sales and career success depend on being able to manage your boss. "Managing up" is a leadership skill that all sales professionals need to perfect to be more motivated and satisfied at work. And a word to you managers out there. If you aren't getting what you need from your team, increases your effectiveness with your own communication development plan. Better communication is the key to fostering good working relationships, effective problem solving and sales success.

<u>*My Managing Up Game Plan*</u>

What will I start or stop doing to communicate better with my manager?

_____

_____

_____

_____

How will we both benefit from better communication?

_____

_____

_____

_____

 Steps/requests I need to make to make these behavior or attitude changes:

1. _____

_____

2. _____

_____

3. _____

_____

CONSULTANTS, NOT SALESPEOPLE, WIN DEALS

"In this world of dramatically changing customer buying behavior and rapidly diverging sales talent, your sales approach must evolve or you will be left behind."

Matthew Dixon & Brent Adamson

Sure Ways to Become a Trusted Advisor

One of my coaching clients, let's call him Ron, was assigned a new enterprise client and his go-to strategy for relationship building was *"getting them to really know me"*. Sadly for Ron and many others sales is not a popularity contest. There is a clear distinction between knowing you and trusting you. Being a trusted advisor is not about convincing clients that you are a wonderful guy or gal but having them feel confident that they are in expert hands.

The role of trusted advisor goes hand in hand with complex, strategic selling today. But what does it really mean and how do the top sales pros earn this coveted title? Truth is there is no fast, 24-hour path to being your client's invaluable resource and partner. It takes commitment, planning and diligence. But the mutual short and long term rewards for both you and the client are well worth the patience and effort. You'll formulate a solid relationship that stands the test of time and endures despite the ups and downs of the business world -- as well as competitors' tactics.

But first it demands a shift in your own mindset from "vendor" to "consultant". Be sure your path to this trusted advisor status includes the following to guarantee success:

- **Become an authority in your industry.** Understand the macro environment better than your competitors and clients. Recognize how these external conditions affect your customer's goals and bottom line.

- **Sweep the corners of the account** to completely grasp customer strategy, priorities and challenges (this is where comprehensive account planning plays a key role!). This means meeting as many contacts as possible -- not just those associated with your potential deals. Include cross functional areas and levels of the account to gain perspective and a reality check from multiple viewpoints. I used to tell customers that a critical component to my job was to understand the Who, What, and Where, When, Why and How of their account. Only then would I be able to make the best use of their time discussing their needs and how I could possibly help.

- **View the world through your customer's eyes.** Remember . . . it's not about you. It's about taking on the perspective of your customer – seeing his business through his eyes and not yours. However, be able to empathize without sympathizing. That is, don't take your understanding to such a point where you identify more closely with their objectives than that of your own organization.

- **Provide insight, not data.** Customers can obtain data any and everywhere today thanks to the internet. What will set you apart is helping clients process the information they've collected by putting it in an appropriate context and using it to co-create a vision to increase their profits and growth. This can indeed be your differential advantage when few exist for your product or service and when it's challenging to pull yourself apart from competitors.

- **Involve your sales team.** Nobody sells complex solutions alone. Help your support team understand the business and financial issues your prospect is experiencing. As a team, develop key insights you can use to up your conversations -

using the collective's in depth product and technical knowledge.

Being a trusted advisor is all about creating real value. Your insights and resulting solutions provide a selling edge that will create customer bonds sure to transcend competitive tactics. Continually ask yourself what you are bringing to the client that they can get nowhere else and that takes them yet another step closer to their success. Their success is your success!

Consider how to expand your role to that of expert advisor at one of your accounts.

 Three actions I will take to make customer conversations more meaningful:

1. _____

_____

2. _____

_____

3. _____

_____

 Steps I need to take to accomplish the above:

1. _____

_____

2. _____

_____

3. _____

_____

Resources or people I need to help me:

1. _____

_____

2. _____

   _____

3. _____

   _____

Ways my new insights & perspective benefit both me and the customer:

1. _____

   _____

2. _____

   _____

3. _____

   _____

Become an Industry Expert to Increase Sales

"An educated customer is the best customer"

Anonymous

As you've read in the previous chapter, vendors are a dime a dozen but turn yourself into an educator and you are singling yourself out for selling complex solutions. Today's buyers are increasingly savvy. Thanks to the internet very often they have already done their homework before ever reaching out to vendors for pricing and demos. So how do you pull yourself apart from the pack by getting involved in the earliest stages of their process? Be the de facto facilitator of their knowledge search. It will help you gain executive access and credibility and put you in the driver's seat to formulate the final solution requirements.

A famous educator once remarked that when you develop a passion for learning, you'll never cease to grow. And your sales will, too! Learning adds an exciting dimension to your work routine and can expand your network with interesting people. Here are some ideas on how to increase your technical competence and become a go-to expert:

Join trade associations. Attend their meetings and seminars and sign up for their blogs, newsletters and webinars.

Brainstorm a list of industry leaders – both internal and external to your organization. Make a point to add these people to your network and develop opportunities to get to know them. Don't be afraid to contact them and with their permission ask questions or for advice. They'll respect you for being a go-getter and generally are happy to share to what they know.

Join LinkedIn groups specific to your industry. Follow and participate in the discussions. Connect and network with other participants.

Read the Wall Street Journal and subscribe to Bloomberg online. No matter what your industry, it's not operating in a bubble. Understand your business from a macro-economic perspective and how your client's own business is affected as well. How are government and monetary policies affecting your industry?

Find resources to increase your own understanding as well as share with clients: white papers, reports, links to websites, and access to other specialists. Make sure the information is purely educational and doesn't contain a pitch for your product or service. It's not having all the answers, but knowing where to find them that's key to building credibility. Customers appreciate that you don't know everything but will search out what they need.

You can also gain trust by **becoming more visible in your industry as a thought leader.** Guest blog, start LinkedIn discussions and volunteer for presentations. If you make your objective not increasing sales per se but becoming an authority, you'll find that opportunities naturally follow.

Finally, your time is money. Acknowledge what it's worth! Employ a win/win strategy early on with your prospect: *"Mr. End User, if I provide* [VALUABLE INDUSTRY INFORMATION/RESOURCES] *to help you make a well- informed decision I will need your help accessing* [MR. DECISION MAKER}. *Is that a reasonable request?"* At the end of the day (sorry, there's that overused phrase!) you need to bring home a sale!

SALES SUCCESS = ATTITUDE + SKILL + TECHNICAL COMPETENCE

Become an expert on your industry!

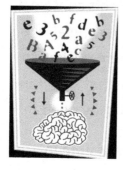
Information sources I'll access to expand industry knowledge:

1. _____

_____

2. _____

_____

3. _____

_____

 What benefits will I & customers derive from my expert status?

1. _____

   _____

2. _____

   _____

3. _____

   _____

DATES & TIMES I will carve into my schedule for learning:

_____

_____

_____

Valuable, knowledge-based business insights based on my research to deliver to clients & prospects:

1. _____

_____

2. _____

_____

3. _____

_____

4. _____

_____

5. _____

_____

Ten Steps to Influence the Executive Suite

Today's top selling account executives are expert at creating long lasting C-Suite relationships based on mutually winning outcomes, understanding and trust. Successfully creating partnerships and gaining influence in the C-suite is a function of discovering and thoroughly comprehending what's important to your client executives. These leaders have a completely different profile from other functional areas within the company that you may sell to like engineering or purchasing. To approach them the same way is sure to tag you "vendor" versus the coveted title "trusted advisor". Maximize your effectiveness by taking on their management perspective and make sure to incorporate these 10 essential steps:

1. **Do your homework!** Get to know as much as possible about your executive and his organization prior to your call or meeting. Online research includes reading and fully comprehending financial statements (footnotes are a great source of information!) and executive bios. Bloomberg, company websites and Google searches for recent

news items are all great sources. Also interview internal coaches and external contacts for insight on your exec's personality and priorities as well as organizational goals and objectives. External contacts may include partners selling into the same account and even former employees you may have in your network.

2. **Obtain a warm reference whenever possible.** It's always better received than a cold call.

3. Executives have heavy schedules and competing priorities. **Respect their time** constraints and the need to end meetings on schedule.

4. **Know their assistants.** They can be a great resource in scheduling and follow up to alleviate "gate keeper" syndrome. Let them know how much you appreciate their help.

5. **Create intimacy** with friendliness, empathy and confidence.

6. **Deliver valuable perspective** that goes well beyond the obvious facts of which executives are aware. Every single conversation needs to convey a comprehensive understanding of your industry as well as the customer's pain points. Asking the

old question, "What's keeping you up at night?" is a sure sign you don't have a clue. The unique perspective that you and your company bring from being highly informed is your differential advantage and makes partnering with you compelling. Instead, offer "_____ *is what we are seeing executives in your role grappling with today. . ."*

7. **Focus on total solutions**, not just the stand alone-benefits your product delivers. Put your product's features in a context that broadens the implications for their entire business.

8. **Co-create vision** that drives results including increasing revenues, reducing costs, time to market, hiring costs, inventories, cost of goods sold or receivables

9. **Rely on data** to drive your points. Senior execs are analytical so have data to back up your claims. Talk in their terms: ROI, ROE, EBITA, etc. If you don't know these terms consider taking a class in basic finance. Every savvy salesperson in complex selling today needs to know how to read a balance sheet and income statement to speak intelligently to the C-level.

10. **Be well prepared** by anticipating questions, possible push back and objections.

One of the biggest mistakes even the most seasoned salespeople make is relying on internal contacts to sell their solutions up the chain or coordinate needed management sign-offs on purchase orders. It's all due to a lack of comfort selling at the top. "Knowledge is power". It builds the confidence you need to hold your own in senior exec conversations. By focusing your attention on the boardroom you'll gain direct access to the ultimate decision makers and signatories in the organization. Imagine the value of this direct relationship not only during the sales process but in developing timelines to negotiate and close your deals faster!

Get to know as much as possible about your C-Level prospect

Sources of information about this executive & his company:

1. _____

   _____

   _____

2. _____

   _____

   _____

3. _____

   _____

   _____

4. _____

   _____

5. _____

_____

_____

What outcome (s) do I want from my first (or next) meeting with this executive?

1. _____

_____

_____

2. _____

_____

_____

3. _____

_____

I will book a meeting with this individual by (DATE):

_____

Resources / people I need to help me get this meeting set:

1. _____

_____

2. _____

_____

3. _____

_____

 Valuable insights based on what I know about their business goals /strategy that I will deliver in the meeting:

1. _____

_____

2. _____

_____

3. _____

_____

TIME MANAGEMENT

In sales, time is money. If you're spending too much of the one you're not making the other!

Anonymous

Organizing Tips for Busy Salespeople

Call me crazy, but being organized brings sheer joy to my days. "Get a life," you may say. But by joy, I mean the happiness that comes when I can find my notes first try or the calmness of walking into a tidy office at the start of my day. Getting and staying organized reduces stress which in turn produces more energy to deal with other mind-bending aspects of my work day. I can hear you from here, "Yeah, must be nice if you have the time." Really, de-cluttering and organization are not as elusive as you may think. The trick is to make the commitment and specifically carve out the time to get and stay organized. Book the time on your calendar -- perhaps a catch-up afternoon or entire day. At the very least put your phone alarm on 15 minutes at the end of the workday to put things in their place.

Here are some other tips for you, too, to become and stay organized:

- Marilyn Paul's book, **"It's Hard to Make a Difference When You Can't Find Your Keys"** is not your typical self-help, "let's get organized" book. It offers a 7 step development program that delves into the personal obstacles to organization. Reading the book helped me create and now maintain a clean desk for the first time in my career. Now when I sit to work I feel invigorated instead of overwhelmed.

- A useful website called Get Buttoned Up: http://getbuttonedup.com. You can sign up for free tools, resources and download printables to help put your life in order. Other tools include a newsletter, blog and products to assist you.

- Don't know where to start? Brainstorm ("brain dump"!) all the areas of your work or home life that are discombobulated and are sucking the very energy out of your days in little ways. Messy handbags in which you can't find the ringing phone, misplaced Post-It notes, a car that looks like you are living in it full time, etc. Choose the top one to three of your brain dump that if addressed would make the biggest difference in your life. Make the commitment to tackle them!

Recently I tackled a master bedroom closet that became an ever growing mess. It took an entire week of my free time but now every time I walk in I am in heaven! I ridded the closet of all the tired clothing, repainted dinged up walls, bought more decorative storage baskets, new rug, scented shelf paper and new hangers. No more precious time crawling on the floor to find shoes, dealing with wrinkled workout clothes or "missing" tops that slipped off hangers onto the floor. I even posted wall art over the door with an inspirational message. My day now begins in an area that's a true energy creator and I can easily find whatever I need in mere seconds!

The top energy drainer from my big brain dump that I will work on right now is:

I will have this resolved or fixed by (DATE): _____

People, tools or resources I need to help me:

1. _____

_____

2. _____

_____

3. _____

_____

 The very first step I need to take to accomplish my goal:

_____

_____

Next steps:

1. _____

_____

2. _____

_____

3. _____

_____

Procrastinating? How To Jumpstart Any Project!

Spring may be the season of growth and renewal. But anytime is perfect to tackle an annoying project that's become sidelined. Clear out your mental cobwebs, get motivated to take action and let the sun shine in!

The consequences of not moving forward likely make your task bigger or more complex. On the other hand, how will you feel when your languishing action item is finally completed? That answer should be enough to get you going. Write down the feelings and benefits you'll create and post them where you can refer to them often.

Pinpoint your goal. What *exactly* do you want to accomplish and why? For example, "Better organizing my contact list" becomes "Prioritizing my contact list by opportunity size".

Determine the actual the scope of the task and how committed you are to getting it done. Be sure your goal is not only measurable and achievable but that you've made a firm resolution to get it done. Without commitment the goal is going nowhere fast.

Start small. Rome wasn't built in a day and 10,000 digital photos can't be organized in a night. Break your project down into smaller, manageable parts and execute in baby steps. Maybe your photos can be organized a single folder at a time. Or use a timer. Spending a mere 30 minutes at a time cleaning your desk is less intimidating than trying to organize the whole office in a single swoop. Seeing immediate results is motivating and will propel you to next steps towards completion.

Create a reasonable timeline. Formulate sensible dates for milestones and completion to keep you on track. Put these dates on your calendar where they can be easily referenced. Making yourself accountable is essential to reaching your target.

Assess Resources. What exactly do you need to reach your goals? Having the proper supplies not only makes your work easier but more fun. Colorful bins or paint? Well-organized folders? Make a list of what's required and purchase if necessary.

Enlist the support of others. Pay your teen for filing those huge piles of documents accumulated on your office floor over the winter. Or ask your spouse to take the kids on a Saturday to free up some time. Let others know your aim and you may be surprised at the help you can muster. Reach out and ask.

Make the process fun! Find creative ways to enjoy the time spent like listening to music or rewarding yourself at completion of a step. Discovering even small ways to appreciate the experience ensures you stay on course.

Ridding yourself of tolerations is liberating and energy producing. There's no better time to "clean house" and enhance your life or work. A well-defined goal broken into easy to digest pieces and done with a positive outlook creates momentum to get that pesky job done!

Okay, okay . . . I have been putting this
[PROJECT/TASK/ACTION/TOLERATION] off in a big way:

_____

_____

_____

_____

_____

_____

What are the unfortunate
consequences of not getting this
done?

1. _____

_____

2. _____

_____

3. _____

   _____

How I will feel when this task or project is completed:

1. _____

   _____

2. _____

   _____

3. _____

   _____

 If I were to break this project into smaller parts, what would they be?

1. _____

2. _____

3. _____

4. _____

5. _____

6. _____

7. _____

I will complete this project by (DATE):

_____

_____

 Who and what do I need to help me?

1. _____

_____

2. _____

_____

3. _____

_____

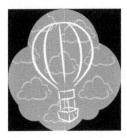 How I can make doing this project more fun?

1. _____

_____

2. _____

   _____

3. _____

   _____

Productivity Killer - Email

You know the scenario. You're at the office at 8AM and what's the first thing you do? Check email of course! It's downhill from there. Before you realize, it's 11AM and you haven't made a dent in the day's projects. So easy to get sucked in! The good news is that it's just as easy to regain control of your workday. With some simple and effective habits you can manage your email instead of allowing it to manage you. You'll find it indeed possible to handle the tsunami of digital communications while remaining on top of it all.

Don't start the day answering email. It's the perfect distraction from crucial projects. Instead, spend your first hour tackling the day's to-do list. Getting a jump on your primary projects will help you feel better about finishing them and give you a quick sense of accomplishment.

Schedule specific times to review incoming emails and stick to it (i.e. 3 times a day for an hour). Prioritize time-sensitive emails and avoid becoming distracted with the non-urgent, non-important ones.

Create an automated email reply that provides your cell number for urgent requests. *"Thank you for your email. If your need is urgent, please call me on my cell: XXX-XXX-XXX. Otherwise I will reply at my earliest opportunity."* Setting expectations for senders takes the pressure off having to reply the minute you read an email.

Create a filter to file emails on which you are cc'd. They'll never even make it to your inbox.

Opt for phone calls. This adds diversity and a more personal touch to communications. It also gives a welcome break away from the computer.

Take technology breaks. Have a backup at the office help with urgent email while on vacation and reciprocate. Peers appreciate the ability to holiday knowing that you are expertly covering for them as well.

Avoiding the daily email time sink is certain to help you proactively manage your day – creating more time and energy for getting other important tasks done.

Three things to start or stop doing immediately and better manage my email:

1. _____

_____

_____

2. _____

_____

_____

3. _____

_____

_____

DRIVING EVEN GREATER RESULTS

"I do not think there is any other quality so essential to success of any kind as the quality of perseverance. It overcomes almost everything . . ."

John D. Rockefeller

You're the Sales Team Quarterback

Account managers never sell complex solutions alone. Whether you're backed by sales engineers, specialists, inside sales people or back office support, it's critical you play the role of quarterback for maximum sales and customer impact. Many sales coaching clients come to me frustrated by customer meetings with their sales team that went seriously adrift. Although it's easier to play the blame game, at the end of the day as the account manager you're the one throat to choke.

It's your job as the sales leader to make absolutely certain that your team understands the client's business needs and perspective and direct them accordingly. Who hasn't s squirmed through a presentation in which team mates droned on to a prospect totally disengaged because the message wasn't tailored to his requirements? Truth is, the sales process has evolved yet many sales teams haven't kept up. Power point presentations won't cut the mustard unless they're adapted to where your customer is in His buying cycle — not yours. One sales meeting or demo that misses the mark and you may never get another opportunity.

Instead, build customer trust in your expertise and commitment to your solution with a well thought out book of plays.

Develop a clear, concise pre-call plan with your team of specialists in advance.

- Include a specific, objective you co-create as a team given the stage of the process The Customer is in as well as his role in the decision.

- Clearly agree upon your objective and strategy as a group.

- Foster buy-in and accountability of individual team members.

- Follow up by having your team rehearse their presentation. This gives you the opportunity to coach them on better positioning, more appropriate verbiage or a more refined customer view.

- Be prepared to remind your support team early and often as to expectations. Better to over communicate requirements than to make assumptions that they have fully digested the information. The last thing you want is a sales engineer bulldozing a business contact with hard to comprehend technical information!

And although it's easy to get discouraged by a meeting that missed the mark (especially after all the preparation!), help team mates learn with post call analysis. Channel your likely irritation into valuable coaching. Sometimes, it takes multiple efforts for a team to truly "get" the sales perspective.

Remember that as an account manager, you are the quarterback. You don't have to play the individual positions yourself, but you do need to lead and direct the plays to create momentum that wins the game.

See Selling Tools and Resources Page for a Call Plan Template

Don't Make These
Top 10 Sales Mistakes!

In my sales coaching practice I see many a sales process that needs tweaking. Here's my list of *Top 10 Sales Mistakes* based on what most often bogs my clients down. You'll find that these are common companions to anemic pipelines and longer sales cycles. How many on the list below sound a bit too familiar?

1. **Waiting too long to follow up** when faced with unreturned calls or emails. I had one coaching client who used to wait a full 2 weeks. A sure-fire way to lose momentum! A two business day wait is tops for a reply depending on how busy you know the contact is.

2. **Failing to solidly establish value** based on your solution at the onset of the sales cycle. Otherwise, is it any wonder that your customer's final negotiations come down to price?

3. **Selling at your comfort level.** Failing to engage executive decision makers leaves you at a complete disadvantage to influencing buying outcomes. Don't expect your contact to sell up the chain on your behalf.

4. **Not completely understanding your customer's business or buying stage.** If you can't tie your solution back to the customer's business pains as well as corporate objectives and strategies or match your selling tactics to their stage in the process you might as well have "Just Another Vendor" taped to your forehead. Recent research suggests that 90% of salespeople fail at connecting the buyer's challenges to their solutions.

5. **Submitting your proposal . . . And waiting . . . and waiting** . . . and waiting. Killing time until a customer gets back to you is not a strategy for closing a deal.

6. **Not committing sacred time for prospecting.** As a result, this critical, on- going sales activity gets relegated behind "checking my email for the 14th time today" or better yet, "too busy closing deals".

7. **Confusing being busy with being productive.** Business hours should be allocated to 80% revenue producing activity. See above!

8. **Not leveraging resources.** This includes your business network, management and specialists as well as sales support and internal tools such as

white papers and research. No successful salesperson is a lone wolf. So learn to delegate and where find answers.

9. **Not keeping up with your industry and trends** because you are "too busy selling". Knowledge is power and it's what going to set you apart as a trusted advisor.

10. **Not taking a vacation** because the business and customers can't live without you. They can - and they do. Even the most productive manufacturing lines must go down for maintenance periodically. Take care of the machinery - you!

The worst mistake, however, is not adjusting your or your team's behavior to be more effective, create more pipeline and close more deals. It's too easy to get into a style rut or lose focus on the very basics of sales success. A coach or manager who is as committed to your sales results as you are will help you leverage your strengths, discover opportunities for growth and ditch the habits that no longer serve you.

 A major selling mistake I am currently making:

_____

_____

_____

<u>Refer to the Success Plan Template on page 13 to formulate your action plan!</u>

Brainstorm Your Way through Sales Snags

Where can I get more warm referrals? What can I do to increase customer touch points? If you've ever had a sales challenge for which you were stuck for answers, you know the benefits of brainstorming. Mind mapping takes this productive exercise and allows you to better organize ideas for greater efficiency in decision making. This useful, but surprisingly little-used tool can have a notable impact on your sales strategies.

Mind mapping allows users to create an outline of information in a visual format. Ideas can then be documented, understood and conveyed to your sale manager, team and even customers more effectively. These visual aids can also be very motivating and fun. They break the cycle of brainstorming tedium found in most offices and training classes.

The mind mapping advantage is further described by the likes of by Litemind (www.litemind.com), a company that explores ways to better use our brains touting that "The power lies in its simplicity". In fact, mind mapping can be as simple or as complex as you decide. Although there are several great software packages and apps available all one needs is pencil and paper. Maps take the form of a spider diagram. Start with the subject you want to explore, and draw spokes from this central idea. These spokes contain related ideas which in turn spawn others - shooting off like branches on a tree. Continue on and on with related ideas which in turn are drawn as additional branches from their own parent topics - until you feel you have exhausted your thoughts.

Mind mapping is certain to get your creative juices flowing and provide a clearer path for thinking out a sales challenge. This helps you more quickly problem solve
- gaining focus and needed insight. Drawing a map is super easy and is described in greater detail on the **Litemind** website. Be sure to do an internet search for more free tools and variations as well.

I like the old pen and paper method and keep my graphs in a notebook (in any event keep your map handy for easy reference). For me, manipulating the various styles of software programs is a distraction from creating better ideas and content. I was so busy making my graph pretty that I wasn't getting much done. For a small fee easy to edit PowerPoint templates such as the one following may be downloaded on Slideshop.com.

Regardless of the format you choose, mind mapping can help you develop new selling strategies and it makes a tedious process more enjoyable and inspiring!

Have fun!

SAMPLE MIND MAP

Mind map your own sales challenges using this
simple template:

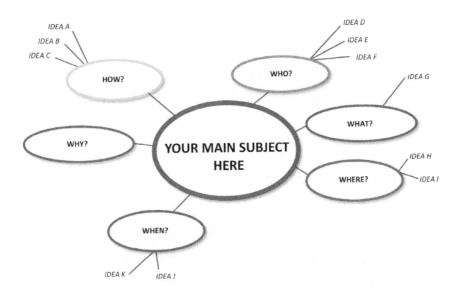

Taken with permission from Slideshop.com

Be Your Own Performance Coach Every Day

Monday Night Football doesn't end with the final score. The game just isn't complete without the witty, insightful, and most of all critical, post-game analysis of ESPN's Mike and Mike. They review the pre-game strategies, decisions made on the field and resulting plays and scoring. It's our sneak peek into how players and coaches analyze various elements and outcomes by focusing attention on the play details. Post-game, players and teams then revise strategy to avoid repeating costly mistakes, continue working on the winning plays and practice drills to ensure greater success next game.

Top strategic account managers also share this process of self-critiquing their abilities, committing to needed changes, evaluating consequences and planning future efforts in line with achieving their goals. It's a constant work in progress. But continual self-examination is critical to staying on top of one's game and achieving maximum business performance. So start assessing your own daily sales game for even greater business and career impact. Learn how to be your own Monday morning quarterback by asking yourself some critical questions at the end of a busy work day:

- **What went well?** Take stock of the day's accomplishments and what you did skillfully. There's always a tendency to focus on the piles of unfinished business left on the desk at 5 P.M. Instead, reflect on what you've completed. What steps did it take to get there? Congratulate yourself on your results and make a commitment to continue in this manner going forward. Recognize and acknowledge both your strengths and opportunities from which you can profit. Appreciating your talents and what is going well helps keep a positive outlook – keeping you motivated for making changes in other areas of development.

- **What did you hope to achieve - but didn't?** Be honest in your assessment of what you could be doing to better manage your selling activities and schedule. What got you off track? How will you execute differently? Think of the specific actions you'll need to take tomorrow to get you to completion. Try keeping an hour by hour time log to see how you're spending your day and identify time wasters. Set limits on meetings, emails and other potential distractions to make sure the way you are spending your time is in line with what you need to get done.

- **Mistakes made?** Reframe them as learning experiences and identify a positive take-away. Be patient with yourself and aim your sight on the destination – not the bump in the road. Or, are you doing the same thing over and over again expecting different results? Albert Einstein observed this behavior as *"the definition of insanity"*. Think about this quotation for a moment.   Is this applicable to you? If so, make a commitment to excellence and the changes needed to propel you forward.

- **Are you absolutely clear about your priorities?** Focus on the projects, pending sales and related to-dos that are both important and urgent. Keep an eye on those important, but not yet urgent, as they will soon enough be on this A-list. And finally, don't waste time on tasks that are neither relevant nor time sensitive. Remember, goals need to be measurable, achievable and results orientated. Make sure yours are meaningful, term, effect on emotions. The simple act of smiling can alleviate some stress and get you over a hump in making progress.

Hold yourself accountable each and every day. Doing your personal best and reaching your fullest sales and business potential is likely when you choose to take action. So consider expanding the opportunity for tomorrow's success with this daily, post-game analysis. Commit to becoming your own cheerleader - as well as your toughest critic. Playing back the day's game tape in your mind, congratulating, critiquing and making changes will bring lasting solutions to your account management obstacles. With this end of day self-review you are certain to execute skillful ways that results in a winning season - increasing sales, profitability and income.

realistic and motivating. Visualize what you are going to achieve tomorrow. Write your goals down and post in several spots where you can be reminded of them throughout your day – on the bathroom mirror, the car dashboard, or your computer.   Being ever reminded of your primary intentions for the day will close the gap between your current and the required outcomes.

- **What skills or tools do you need** to reach your sales goals? If you could wave a magic wand and morph yourself into a model for your job what would that look like? How would you physically look and act? Hour by hour, what are the things you'd be doing? Write down your description of the ultimate workday and yourself as a top strategic account manager. What skills or tools are needed to create this image? Research best practices and learn from other top producers in your company. Who is executing in a way to which you aspire? What are they doing right? What qualities can you emulate and what tools can you, too, obtain? Consider getting a mentor or coach who has the experience and qualities you desire and engage them for quick, end of day discussions a few times a week. Research has verified that mentoring and coaching can have positive impacts on job performance.

In addition, there are many skills inventories available (see the Selling Resources page) or ask your manager or a sales coach to help you identify areas of development if you are unsure. Put a plan together for improvement that might include in-person classes, webinars, self-study and books. Much is offered through colleges or professional or industry organizations and their websites. The most successful strategic account managers are committed to lifelong learning – adding knowledge and skills to ensure top performance and career advancement. Make sure you, too, are integrating time for development into your schedule.

- **What habits support your game plan for tomorrow?** Get out of your own way by practicing habits in line with your values and purpose. Decide on daily personal (i.e. get up earlier) or business habits (i.e. create tomorrow's to-do list before leaving office) that you want to introduce or keep and make a list of 10. Create a spreadsheet or table and check off whether you are accomplishing the habit each day. Celebrate your successes. And remember, it takes 3- 6

months of continual practic
Don't try and develop new
"should". If yours aren't ch
your commitment and repl
on your list.

- **Do you have a winning at**
reality every day with pos
you are capable of achiev
leads to positive thinking
success. Put another wa
people tend to expect wi
they do. A positive attitu
and more productive, ge
and earning higher inco
confident. These people
work on for longer peri
therefore more likely t
the repeating of a man
expecting the best nee
aspect of your day. To
outlook focus on that
control, surround you
grateful for existing o
frustrated, smile. Re
smiling does indeed I

My Daily Performance Self-Analysis Worksheet

What did I accomplish today?

_____

_____

_____

What did I intend to complete but didn't? Is it a real priority?

_____

_____

_____

What challenges or problems am I facing now?

_____

_____

_____

_____

What opportunities are available to me ht now?

_____

_____

_____

realistic and motivating. Visualize what you are going to achieve tomorrow. Write your goals down and post in several spots where you can be reminded of them throughout your day – on the bathroom mirror, the car dashboard, or your computer. Being ever reminded of your primary intentions for the day will close the gap between your current and the required outcomes.

- **What skills or tools do you need** to reach your sales goals? If you could wave a magic wand and morph yourself into a model for your job what would that look like? How would you physically look and act? Hour by hour, what are the things you'd be doing? Write down your description of the ultimate workday and yourself as a top strategic account manager. What skills or tools are needed to create this image? Research best practices and learn from other top producers in your company. Who is executing in a way to which you aspire? What are they doing right? What qualities can you emulate and what tools can you, too, obtain? Consider getting a mentor or coach who has the experience and qualities you desire and engage them for quick, end of day discussions a few times a week. Research has verified that mentoring and coaching can have positive impacts on job performance.

In addition, there are many skills inventories available (see the Selling Resources page) or ask your manager or a sales coach to help you identify areas of development if you are unsure. Put a plan together for improvement that might include in-person classes, webinars, self-study and books. Much is offered through colleges or professional or industry organizations and their websites. The most successful strategic account managers are committed to lifelong learning – adding knowledge and skills to ensure top performance and career advancement. Make sure you, too, are integrating time for development into your schedule.

- **What habits support your game plan for tomorrow?** Get out of your own way by practicing habits in line with your values and purpose. Decide on daily personal (i.e. get up earlier) or business habits (i.e. create tomorrow's to-do list before leaving office) that you want to introduce or keep and make a list of 10. Create a spreadsheet or table and check off whether you are accomplishing the habit each day. Celebrate your successes. And remember, it takes 3- 6 months of continual practice to make a habit stick. Don't try and develop new habits because you "should". If yours aren't changing, reevaluate your commitment and replace or adjust the habit on your list.

- **Do you have a winning attitude?** Make your own reality every day with positive self-talk about what you are capable of achieving. Positive self-talk leads to positive thinking which is essential to success. Put another way, high-productivity people tend to expect winning outcomes in what they do. A positive attitude makes people happy and more productive, gets them promoted faster and earning higher incomes than those less confident. These people set higher goals that they work on for longer periods of time, and are therefore more likely to attain. But it's beyond the repeating of a mantra. A prevailing mindset of expecting the best needs to permeate every aspect of your day. To maintain an optimistic outlook focus on that which is under your direct control, surround yourself with winners and be grateful for existing opportunities. When you are frustrated, smile. Recent studies suggest that smiling does indeed have a positive, albeit short-term, effect on emotions. The simple act of smiling can alleviate some stress and get you over a hump in making progress.

- **Hold yourself accountable each and every day.** Doing your personal best and reaching your fullest sales and business potential is likely when you choose to take action. So consider expanding the opportunity for tomorrow's success with this daily, post-game analysis. Commit to becoming your own cheerleader - as well as your toughest critic. Playing back the day's game tape in your mind, congratulating, critiquing and making changes will bring lasting solutions to your account management obstacles. With this end of day self-review you are certain to execute skillful plays that results in a winning season - increasing sales, profitability and income.

What will I do differently tomorrow?

_____

_____

_____

What news skills or tools do I
need? How will acquire them?

1. _____

_____

2. _____

_____

3. _____

_____

 How am I going to stay focused and on task tomorrow?

_____

_____

_____

_____

_____

Create 10 Daily Habits to Increase Your Sales

Post-It notes all over your desk, overdue client follow up, double booked meetings . . . How can you possibly sell more juggling an already hefty workload? In spite of the chaos, it's possible to create more energy, focus and close more sales. The answer is to create daily rituals that support your direct selling efforts.

According to Merriam-Webster Online (www.merriam-webster.com), a habit is *"an acquired mode of behavior that has become nearly or completely involuntary."* Good habits are the backbone of high performers — rituals practiced routinely become engrained in the day and create traction for more sales. Make sure you're executing to increase sales by determining activities you can implement every day to be more productive and focused:

- Decide on 10 daily tasks that will increase or make more effective your face-to face selling time. Some examples: update CRM database at the end of each day, enter notes and follow ups right after each customer contact, establish a minimum number of client meetings per day, schedule specific times to formulate call plans or to make cold calls, etc. Habits need to be detailed, achievable and fun. Keep them fairly simple and visualize yourself executing and increasing your sales. If tasks are too complicated or you can't imagine yourself more successful as a result they are less likely to get acted upon.

- Write your new daily rituals on a chart where you can track them for a week. Check off each day the item you successfully completed.
- Find a model sales person or manager who has the practices you wish to imitate. They may even be inclined to mentor you in making the needed changes.
- Make a month long commitment as change doesn't occur overnight. It takes approximately 6 weeks for new behaviors to take hold. Be patient and mark your calendar to check progress. If you deviate from your goals give yourself some slack and commit to trying again tomorrow.
- See how many habits and days you checked off each week and be sure to celebrate your accomplishments.

- Reassess if you are consistently not executing on one of your desired habits. Consider tweaking or replacing it with one more in line with your needs.

A list of 10 daily personal habits can also be made to contribute to an overall sense of well-being. These activities may be related to your physical environment, personal growth, relationships, health, money or leisure. Long-term business success is also a function of self-care. When you feel good you are going to have the energy to keep this renewed sales focus.

Armed with top 10 daily selling habits you'll close more deals by focusing on revenue-generating priorities. Repeat these behaviors so often that they become part of the very fabric of your workday and you'll be well on your way to more customers and commissions!

10 DAILY HABITS SCORING SHEET: List habits & check off daily. Good Luck!

My Daily Habit	Check off each day you complete your new habit:						
	Mon	Tue	Wed	Thu	Fri	Sat	Sun
1.							
2.							
3.							
4.							
5.							
6.							
7.							

8.							
9.							
10.							

If I Only Had A Better Territory!

Some of the most successful salespeople have territories they aren't thrilled about. Perhaps they've been assigned accounts owned by the competition, customers lacking budget or an unrealistic quota. You can be like my former colleague who monopolized every sales meeting with complaints about how things should be. Or, you can take a tip from top sales performers and make it happen!

Don't fall into playing the blame game or making excuses this year. Consider that the most successful salespeople have winning attitudes, the highest levels of personal initiative and responsibility and are persistent. They research and reach out to customers with a plan regardless of circumstances. Here are some strategies to help if you're in a funk:

- **First, clear your mind of all negative thinking.** Consider how you can you reframe your situation into a positive. Successful salespeople have a knack for redefining the seemingly impossible into an opportunity that they can then tackle with enthusiasm. For example, *"My largest account* *has no budget so won't buy anything this year."* becomes *"How can I co-develop with my client a plan for deferring payment to avoid using capital this year?"*

Or *"Account X never rents – they only buy"* translates to opportunity as in, *"How can I show Account X the value of renting and how it helps them meet their [financial, sales, research, etc.] goals?"*

- **Be committed to results and accountable to a success plan.** Don't use the "bad account" label as an excuse for avoiding sales activities like prospecting or addressing the competition. Low performers often expect the business to come straight at them instead of taking the initiative to go after it with cold calling and face to face meetings. If you don't leave your office trying to live off of low hanging fruit and waiting for the phone to ring you'll certainly fail in the long run.

- **Let go of issues that are outside of your control.** Successful salespeople focus on the factors under their direct influence. Dwelling on what you can't control saps valuable energy.

- **Assess your sales skills and technical competence** — both key ingredients to greater confidence and successfully overcoming your current situation. Seek out resources and tools from your training department, management or industry associations to help you fill in skill gaps and add to your knowledge base.

- When all else fails and your quota is indeed based on some faulty crystal ball prediction, **develop with your manager what your success will *really* look like for the year and a plan of action.** It may be that attaining a percentage of goal or reaching certain MBOs becomes the de facto target. Remember that life and sales quotas aren't always fair.

- **Be creative.** Think outside the box for strategy. I received a Team Leadership Award for a multimillion dollar lease to a Fortune 100 client with a strict corporate mandate, *"We don't lease"*. It can happen!

Join the successful salespeople who don't worry about *if* they make goal this year but *when*. Mapping out a solid game plan to combat territory challenges puts you on a path to succeed!

Develop Your Winning Strategy

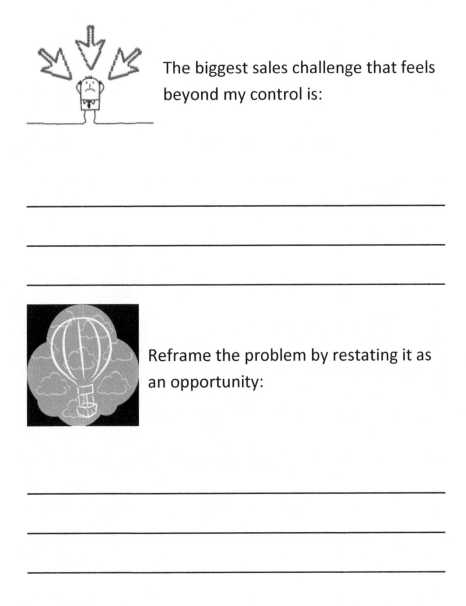

The biggest sales challenge that feels beyond my control is:

_____

_____

_____

Reframe the problem by restating it as an opportunity:

_____

_____

_____

 Three (3) immediate steps I can take to address this situation:

1. _____

2. _____

3. _____

The benefit(s) of my success:

_____

_____

_____

 What I aim to lose if nothing changes:

_____

_____

_____

People or tools I can tap to help me reach my goals:

1. _____

2. _____

3. _____

Top 10 Characteristics of Successful Salespeople

Sales success calls for the right mix of mindset, heart and skills. What are the solid six figure income earners doing and how can you join their ranks? Exam your own qualities and see how you match up!

Check off and see how many of these traits you have:

- ✓ **Persistence.** Calvin Coolidge remarked, "*Nothing in the world can take the place of Persistence*". In an environment where sales cycles are more complex, persistence pays. The successful salesperson remains diligently engaged so she can take advantage of opportunities internal or external to her prospects. So discover techniques to stay involved with your prospects despite their present reluctance to do business.

- ✓ **Expert listening skills.** Rain makers ask quality questions to thoroughly understand the client's organization and priorities. . . And then sit back and listen. Being fully attentive, they clearly grasp a customer's goals and can then craft conversation and solutions that provide important insight.

✓ **Ability to create value**. The big guns don't allow themselves to become vulnerable to always playing defense to get their deals. **Establishing clear** customer **value** up front gives them a solid position even when a competitor's price is lower. Discover how to create worth in your solution that transcends cost. You don't need to rely on having the lowest price to get the deal!

✓ **Focus**. When asked, most salespeople rank more selling time over a need for leads. Skillful salespeople avoid the time sinks that distract from direct contact with quality leads and customers. So develop plans for managing your time, territory and administrative tasks.

✓ Being **relationship versus transaction based**. Talented salespeople sell past an individual deal or opportunity by becoming trusted advisors who craft valuable customer-centric solutions, not just reps pushing product. So acquire methods that forge relationships yielding long term, repeat business.

✓ **Being accountable** for results. Winning salespeople don't play the blame game. They own the results. So improve self-management to be totally reliable for reaching your goals — in spite of external factors.

✓ **Passion**. Passion stems from a sincere love of industry and product. It's a source of motivation and goes hand in hand with success. If your heart isn't into what you are doing, do everyone a favor and consider making a change to an industry or product that truly excites you.

✓ **Goal-orientated**. Great salespeople can visualize the end result – and go for it. Use the techniques in previous chapters to craft solid plans for achieving your goals. Plan your work and work your plan to get what you want.

✓ **Enthusiasm** about the sales process itself. Mindset is as important as skillset when it comes to selling. Discover ways to get motivated and excited about your daily tasks including the more mundane. With eagerness comes energy that is critical for enduring long hours and overcoming reluctance. Motivated and successful salespeople understand that with hard work comes much reward.

✓ **Resourcefulness**. Top performers don't necessarily have all the answers but they do know where to find them. Explore ways to be creative (did someone say *"mind map"*?) when up against obstacles and think beyond the obvious answers. Learn to network well with others who know more than you do and go to school on them.

There is indeed a tried and true recipe to sales success. It's not, as they say, rocket science. But it does take a commitment to develop the right attitude and skills. Commit to these top performance traits and you, too, can become a wildly successful sales star!

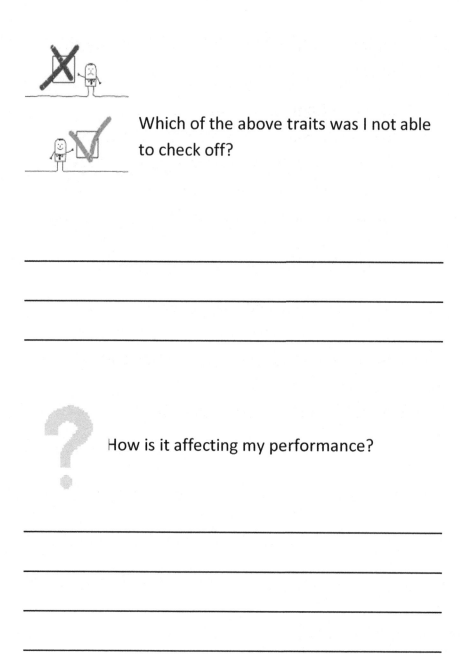

Which of the above traits was I not able to check off?

_____

_____

_____

How is it affecting my performance?

_____

_____

_____

_____

_____

_____

_____

_____

_____

What would be the direct benefit in acquiring this trait?

_____

_____

_____

_____

_____

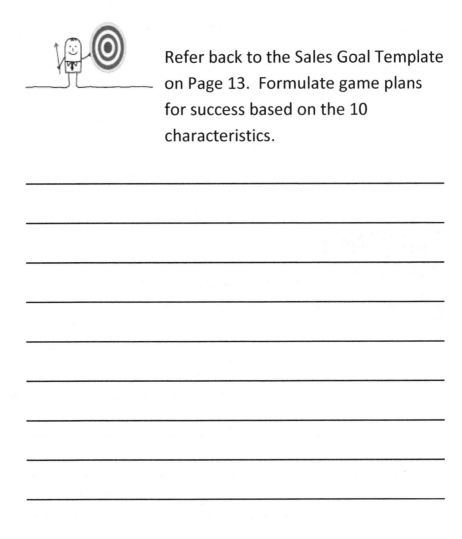

Refer back to the Sales Goal Template on Page 13. Formulate game plans for success based on the 10 characteristics.

_____

_____

_____

_____

_____

_____

_____

_____

_____

Mentors Are a Must

It's challenging at best. You do all the right things to grow your business including marketing, social and in-person networking and calls to decision makers. Yet you're working very long days and not seeing results for all this dedication and commitment. Feeling like a gerbil on a wheel, you can't find needed momentum to get your business in gear for greater revenues. What do you do?

Mentoring is a great option for young salespeople and seasoned business owners alike. Mentors enjoy helping others and sharing their own successes. They bring to the table a perfect blend of coaching and consulting. This is done by their listening and asking the right questions to help you arrive at your own answers to overcoming business obstacles. At the same time they lend invaluable experience and expertise to also provide solutions.

Mentors help people who help themselves, though. They are not going to do the necessary actions for you — but enjoy acting as a guide to educate and advise.

Some of the most accomplished Silicon Valley business people have had mentors including Steve Jobs at Apple. Seventy percent of Fortune 500 companies have mentoring programs.   And if you own a small company there are government resources that are available.

Finding a mentor on your own takes time and work. Mentors may be found in in person and social media networking groups as well as professional and industry organizations. Most winning mentor relationships grow out of an existing connection or personal referral, though. So leverage successful business contacts. Who do you know that is truly interested in you? Find someone you trust who is wildly successful in a similar business. Take them out to lunch and don't be shy in asking for support. Remember that key to acquiring and keeping a mentor is having them acutely aware of all your hard work and motivation. It's a real benefit if they have already been witnessing first-hand your efforts to get results.

Drive and ambition are paramount in growing your business in a competitive and challenged market. Complementing with a mentor who provides solid support and cheerleading can propel you to new levels in achieving your goals.

How would support of a mentor help me?

1. _____

_____

2. _____

_____

3. _____

_____

Successful people I know who may want to mentor me:

1. _____

_____

2. _____

_____

3. _____

   _____

Places I can find other potential mentors:

1. _____

   _____

2. _____

   _____

3. _____

   _____

I will find a mentor and schedule time with them by (DATE):

MOTIVATION

"It is our attitude at the beginning of a difficult task which, more than anything else, will affect its successful outcome."

William James

Help for the War Weary

Meet Claudia. She's 55, has been with the same technology company for a dozen years and handles a single large client. Years of hard work have yielded robust relationships but account opportunities just aren't coming the way they used to. Claudia was always an invaluable part of the team. However, ask Claudia and she'll tell you that she tired of the weekly non-stop travel and long hours. The income's been great and she's accomplished wonderful things in her personal life including getting her boys through college on a single income, buying the house of her dreams and living an enviable lifestyle. But internally Claudia is restless as she grapples with what's become a daily grind. Should she change business units? Sock enough away and pursue her life-long desire for travel? Ask for another account that may present more of a challenge? Or even consider a second career as she's always thought about being a high school teacher?

I've been coaching sales executives exactly like Claudia who are mature in their careers with years of experience and much strategic account training behind them. However, they are no longer cutting the mustard -

plagued with sagging quota attainment as their sales environment shifts in ways foreign to them. Focus swings from building to sustaining success. Many of these senior account executives are increasingly frustrated for a variety of internal and personal reasons among which may be a lack of what to do to address changing tides.

"Go in the direction of your dreams and live the life you've imagined"

<u>If you find yourself in a funk here are some useful activities:</u>

 What personal strengths do I credit for past sales success?

1. _____

2. _____

3. _____

 What's changed since my days of wild success?

_____

_____

_____

 What selling behaviors are no longer producing the results they did in the past? Why not?

1. _____

_____

2. _____

_____

3. _____

   _____

So what behaviors changes need do I need to make to adjust to today's selling environment?

1. _____

   _____

2. _____

   _____

3. _____

   _____

4. _____

   _____

What new technology or tools are available to help me?

1. _____

_____

2. _____

_____

3. _____

_____

What will I do to get more information on the above?

1. _____

_____

2. _____

   _____

3. _____

   _____

4. _____

   _____

5. _____

   _____

What are the specific benefits of making needed
behavior changes?

1. _____

   _____

2. _____

   _____

3. _____

   _____

 Identify one thing you can do *right now* to move yourself in the direction of the goals you've identified:

_____

_____

_____

Resources or people who can help you:

1. _____

_____

2. _____

_____

3. _____

   _____

Milestones and (DATES):

_____

_____

_____

Be Present & Enjoy the Moment

One Sunday in church my six year old looked up and asked how old I would be when I died. I replied that I hope to make it to 92 (seemed like a great age) at which time she'd be celebrating her fiftieth birthday. *"Now when you go, are you taking your Blackberry with you?"* Shocked, I got her message loud and clear. She was going to remember me as the mother who always had her nose in her cell phone checking up on work items. Truth is, that's the day I decided to stop working full time which truthfully I'd been contemplating for a while. However, many of us just don't have that luxury.

Life as a working parent is challenging on the very best of days. You ruminate about family while in a meeting and brainstorm work issues while watching the kids play. The constant tug between the two powerful dynamics of work and home life can most often leave you feeling tired, mentally exhausted and disengaged. There is another way. It's possible to abandon this tug of war in favor of greater enjoyment of the many moments that make up your busy day. A wonderful source of inspiration to help you appreciate and enjoy each experience is based on Eckhart Tolle's, **The Power of**

Now: A Guide to Spiritual Enlightenment, New World Library, 2004.

Although in publication for several years, the basis of the book still resonates with those of us juggling hectic schedules.

Ask yourself . . .

- Am I tired of being mentally "on" when it comes to work even when at home supposedly relaxing?
- Do I think about clients, conversations or action items constantly?
- Do I harbor pangs of guilt or anxiety when I must leave the office early for a family commitment? Or vice-versa?
- Am I addicted to constant inputs of information from the internet, social media, T.V or email?

Centering your mind to be "in the moment "can help you appreciate and enjoy what life is gifting you at any particular instant. Letting go of the concept of time and extraneous thought and training yourself to be in the present and truly available for what and whoever is commanding attention creates joy.

B-R-E-A-T-H-E. It's not easy to do and takes some practice.

And the next time your youngster or husband talks to you sit down, give them your full attention and make eye contact. Be there – mentally as well as physically. Turn off the running spigot of thought and allow the world to stop by focusing on what is happening in the present. What you are experiencing and feeling at that instant? On weekends shut your Smartphone off (despite the magnetic pull of social media!). Watch your son's baseball game with a full awareness of sights, sounds and smells. You can't be completely in the present with one eye and hand on your mobile device – no matter how well you think you multitask. Focusing <u>all</u> your attention on what you are presently doing creates mental alertness. You'll find a renewed source of joyful energy in your family and personal activities by immersing yourself entirely in what you are doing and experiencing at any given moment. Your children and spouse will surely notice a transformation from being the distracted parent and partner to one fully engaged.

Energized, you'll be in the right mind when you're back at the office and with your clients. Taking that peace and calm into your business day is certain to help you increase efforts and sales!

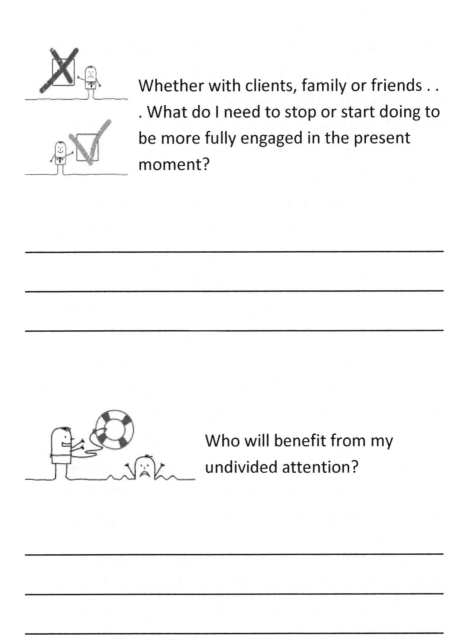

Whether with clients, family or friends . . . What do I need to stop or start doing to be more fully engaged in the present moment?

_____

_____

_____

Who will benefit from my undivided attention?

_____

_____

_____

 How will they benefit?

_____

_____

_____

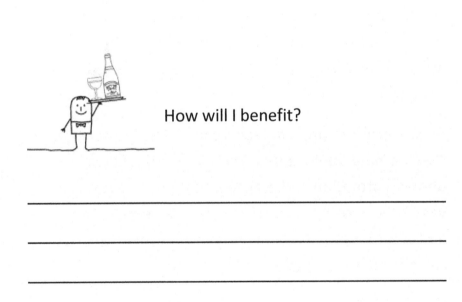 How will I benefit?

_____

_____

_____

Stay Motivated → Increase Sales

Even the most successful salespeople find it hard to stay motivated for years on end. One day you wake up, grab coffee, and drag yourself to your computer and then . . . . Nothing. You find yourself bored to virtual tears contemplating the same contacts, same email requests, and same mouth-gaping sales meetings. Many of us have been there. *"If I have to give this presentation one more time I am going to spit nails!"* I myself shouted in the car one day on the way to a sales call. (Coming to my senses I was relieved to confirm that I was indeed alone. That would have been embarrassing – or career limiting!)

Alas, there's no time in a sales career for this nonsense. As a looming quota stares you in the face, clients demand attention and management needs data — yesterday. Close your eyes . . . . Take a deep breath . . . and create ways to wake from the living dead and start selling with verve again:

Take a REAL vacation — not a day off or a long weekend. The kind of vacation that is free from the demands of technology, people and seven European capitals in seven days (that's travel, not a vacation). You can manage to break away completely when you commit to getting a coverage plan in place at the office.

Change your perspective. Stop yourself from taking things too seriously and find ways to laugh by mentally turning the bombs being lobbed into water balloons. Redefining a situation from a negative to a positive is a powerful tool for regaining focus and energy.

Remember that your job is what you do – not who you are. The company is going to likely be in existence long after you are gone. So schedule on your calendar time to nourish what matters to you personally and spiritually: a noon time Mass, Thursday night out with your spouse, a pre-work run or an hour of volunteer time at your child's school. When you die nobody but your former assistant is going to remember you as "Salesperson of the Year, 20010-2015". Well, okay, maybe she won't either.

Change jobs. The economy is rebounding in sectors and many sales jobs are out there for qualified candidates. (Have you sourced LinkedIn lately?!) One sales consultant friend just found a top notch assignment after looking for only a week. There's never any harm in looking. And if you are planning an exit do just that. Plan whether your move is one year or five years out.

Formulate a strategy and decide on a first step to take to get you moving in that direction. (By the way, this was my ticket to another more stimulating sales position after my shout fest in the car!)

Focus on personal goals to work towards. Saving for a vacation house, buying a boat, affording those pricey skating lessons for your 10 year old Olympian in the making. Post pictures of your goals at your desk to remind yourself of your higher purpose. This "dream board" provides a constant source of inspiration.

Create an energizing oasis with your workspace using fresh flowers, reminders of your hobbies, vacation photos, and the kids' artwork. Invest in accessories that make you feel inspired and successful: an antique vase for a pencil holder, a brass lamp, a Mahogany writing desk. Clean up the clutter. Make your workspace a place that's inviting and you'll actually look forward to more stimulating time spent there.

My Queen Anne, leather topped writing desk oozes "Success", the glass filled jar of Cape Cod sand and shells, "Tranquility" and posted notes from my daughter, "Delight". I can't help but feel creative!

Reward yourself – especially for the more tedious tasks. Despise cold calling? Book them in the morning and do something fun at lunchtime like going for a run or getting manicure. Having something to look forward to (yes, a reward!) does lighten the load.

When you've hit a wall take a tip from expert runners and don't give up. Instead, marathoners pace themselves – often taking walking breaks. High impact salespeople need their breathers, too. Find what works for you . . . even the tempo and re-energize for increasing sales and success long-term.

FOR MANAGERS

"Leaders live by choice, not by accident."

Mark Gorman

Your Communication Style Affects Team Performance

If your salespeople aren't executing either individually or as a team it's easy to point a finger. But as my husband likes to jokingly remind our family, when you point . . . your other four fingers are pointing right back at you. Many of my sales manager clients complain that critical messages to their sales team go unheeded and cause the likes of undocumented sales activities, lack of deal updates, unreliable forecasts, personnel conflicts or unaccounted for time working remotely. If this is true for you, too, then it may be time to examine your communication style and how you are messaging to your salespeople. When it comes to leadership, effective interpersonal skills including oral and written communication are fundamental competencies and key to building sales teams that consistently achieve results.

In evaluating your communication methods consider the following:

- How effectively do you promote the company vision and mission?

- What one-on-one conversations are you having to develop the individuals on your team and how are they producing job satisfaction, motivation, reducing stress and turnover?

- What activities are you executing upon to develop your team as a cohesive unit?

- Do your communications convey a standard of integrity, trust and fairness?

- Do your conversations equally contain empathy as well as strength of conviction?

- How do you respond to problems and challenges?

- How are you dealing with the pace of your environment? Do you react instead of acting with intention in what you say and do?

- In what ways are you fostering individual accountability?

- How successful are you in influencing your salespeople to your or the company point of view?

- How are you setting expectations for rules and procedures?

- How are you advocating for the team when it comes to upper management?

- Does your staff understand your availability and level of support?

Communication style isn't a one size fits all. Adaptive communication style may be needed to match the different personality types on your team. What works well for one may not work with another when it comes to conveying expectations and important information. So explore avenues for further opportunity and growth in your communication skills and that of your entire team. By executing on a commitment to your own communication development you are setting the stage for highly effective leadership especially in time of change — as well as better driving of results that increase sales and revenue.

Identify and calibrate your communication style for maximum performance!

See the Selling Tools and Resources Page to order a Free Talent Insights Report & Debrief.

The Not-So-Shocking Truth about Sales Training

When I was selling for Fortune 100 companies the training departments spent thousands of dollars for skill development and speakers – usually once a year at a kickoff meeting. With a frenzy matched only by the Seattle Seahawk's 12th man, sales managers and account managers alike eagerly listened to tips, copiously took notes on technique, furiously filled out account templates and formulated exciting sales activity goals. No sooner did everyone get back to the office, however, and the all that great learning and enthusiasm quickly began to disappear like the optimism of the Denver Broncos during the first play of Super Bowl XLVVIII. Okay, maybe one or two pearls of wisdom stuck, but for the most part it was business as usual for most of the sales team – the manuals, books and templates surreptitiously stuffed in a credenza only to see daylight during the next office move.

Don't waste your precious training resources. Ongoing training is critical to skill improvement and creating best practices for both new and seasoned sales professionals. On-line or in-person classes and seminars are fundamental "seeing" and "hearing" learning components. Even so, don't expect new information or habits to stick long term without adding a "doing" component. That's where coaching after training plays a critical role.

One-on-one and group coaching set up at regular intervals facilitates your team's ongoing reinforcement of behaviors to increase sales. Make sure sales actually implements changes by setting training-related targets and checking against actual outcomes ensures what has been learned is not lost amid a sea of good intentions and budget dollars spent. Coaching keeps the team accountable for achieving these training goals by helping reps overcome internal and external obstacles. "Doing" is the link that guarantees success and that training money is well invested - leading to increased sales and revenue.

SEEING + LISTENING + DOING = RESULTS

How to Benefit From Leadership Coaching

Complimentary discovery sessions are offered by nearly every executive or leadership coach. This is a great opportunity to "try-on" coaching and boost your management performance. Experience first-hand and without obligation how it can help you and your business achieve results. And if your executive coach doesn't offer a free session? Ask for one!

Being prepared ensures you make the most of this gift of coaching time and talent. So here are tips for benefiting:

1. Be certain your coach has graduated from an approved International Coach Federation (ICF) training program. In addition, **make sure the coach has successful first-hand experience** with your role whether it is entrepreneur, sales or executive. (Would you ever want a business coach who has never owned her own business?!) Retain a leadership coach who has actually walked in your shoes. They're out there . . . and have a context to ensure coaching success.

2. **Be coachable**. Ask yourself, "Is now the *right* time to investigate coaching?" Are you really prepared to make changes? Are you open to adjusting your thinking and trying out new ideas or methods? Can you identify specific business results you want to achieve? Leadership coaching is most successful when the process is linked directly to business results.

3. **Be prepared** for your discovery session with an immediate issue to solve and request 30-60 minute coaching. Experiencing coaching directly helps you grasp how truly effective it can be and how well you and the coach work together.

4. **Be fully present** for your discovery session. Employee interruptions and ringing cell phones make it impossible to get the most out of the conversation. Find a quiet place and clear line for talking if over the phone.

5. **Be honest about your expectations**. Understand whether the coach also mentors and consults. Get clear agreement in the session about potential business, personal and leadership results to help identify if coaching is right for you.

6. **Be ready to take the next step**. Coaches offer these introductory calls to create awareness, and invite you to sign up for ongoing sessions. Leadership coaching rates vary from approximately $500 to thousands per session so know in advance if you are willing to make the investment and time commitment in yourself and your company.

Leadership coaching is powerful in helping you overcome business gaps on all levels by leveraging your strengths and discovering opportunities for team, individual and business growth. A free discovery session benefits by showing first-hand how coaching can help you be a better owner or manager and get your business to the next level.

See Appendix for More Information on FREE Discovery Sessions

Gamification: The Newest Way to Increase Sales

What is Gamification?

Gamification is leading a transformation in how sales forces are engaged at work and with their customers using scalable, dependable often cloud-based technology. Through gamification companies have developed a solution that uses the thinking and mechanics behind web-based games and applied it in a business setting to significantly improve sales productivity. When fun and engaging gaming methods are added sales and training programs are proving more successful. And the results of existing reward programs are being multiplied.

Everyone benefits

The bane of sales management is the age-old challenge of motivating teams in meaningful ways to increase results as well as employee retention. Many of today's salespeople are 20 and 30- something and grew up playing video games – enjoying the fast pace on top of the immediate satisfaction of earning rewards and moving ahead levels. These reps require training and often expect to change jobs as quickly as they flip between apps on their iPhones. On the other end of the spectrum are Baby Boomers in the mature phase of their careers and who are used to time-honored incentives like cash and prizes. Meriting the word "Senior" in their titles means something to them.

Gamification benefits by crossing demographics as all employees share a fundamental human need for recognition. Studies show that satisfying this need indeed creates higher motivation, job satisfaction and employee retention. All people enjoy playing games and they certainly like having a good time. So it makes perfect sense that adding fun and challenge to earning incentives and completing sales activities and training yields even greater motivation.

Companies such as gamification leader Bunchball (www.bunchball.com)offer a platform that is all about people in more general terms and moves them to do what's important. It's estimated that implementation can increase a company's success rate in enterprise application use 50% to 75% as the battle is getting users to actually use it.   It's often easier for salespeople to do nothing. Sales pipelines become in disarray leading to unsatisfied customers. This makes the price of failure to implement very high when one also adds the cost of job dissatisfaction, absenteeism and turnover. The outlays are so much more than actual dollars. And in addition senior sales managers end up fired over the results. Gamification can simply and successfully stimulate desired employee behaviors by making those activities more fun, interactive and stimulating.

Leaders in gamification approach solving a people problem -- not a technology problem. Without employee motivation state of the art enterprise applications become nothing more than a Ferrari without gas!

Accurate Forecasting Out the Gate

A sales manager client remarked that he was so very tired of nagging his reps for their sales forecasts. The lack of accountability to scrub the pipeline for real deals as well as failure to get them in on time was driving him crazy. Each week he found himself stressed knowing that he was rolling a less than reliable forecast up to his own manager. And clearly, theses weak sales forecasts were compromising his credibility and leadership skills.

Sound very familiar? It did to me!

For years as an account manager and now as a sales coach, I see sales teams placating management with hastily thrown together reports so they can go on their merry way to more important matters. The more sales activity documented and submitted the better goes the thinking – no matter the quality. Hey, some of it should actually close! Lesser performing account managers hide behind activity to conceal a lack of real deals – creating false expectations and buying themselves more time. High performers may sandbag deals or hold them over to subsequent periods to level out their quota attainment. Everyone else is giving lip service.

If you're a manager experiencing the angst of unreliable sales projections, here are some strategies to help:

- ✓ Make it a group process. Help salespeople recognize how accurate forecasting benefits them with more executive, marketing and pricing support as this information heads up the chain. If reps are putting garbage in the funnel, they can't expect the right sales support from the organization.

- ✓ Make sure the group fully comprehends factors that affect probabilities for closing as well as the need for relevant data. If your salespeople lack information it may be a sign that they need your coaching.

- ✓ Be perfectly clear about expectations. Most managers receive what they ask for — or don't. Specifically describe the kinds of deals that are at acceptable thresholds for inclusion in the funnel.

- ✓ Set an exact deadline for remittance and revise sales forecasts frequently to keep them current.

- ✓ Establish consequences for non-compliance by make forecasting goals a part of your reps' performance objectives and reviews.

✓ Keep the process as simple as possible. Salespeople are loath to complete administrative tasks. Make this a quick, easy activity using online templates, software and applications. The simpler, the better.

Obtain acknowledgement from salespeople that they understand the advantages of reliable projections, the process itself and the consequences for mismanagement. Getting clear agreement upfront sets the stage for effectively dealing with lapses in cooperation by holding them to what they signed up for and why. Finally, give your reps something in return like allocating them the time to do the forecast properly. Your support in helping them help you will be appreciated.

 What's my biggest complaint about my team's current forecasting?

_____

_____

_____

 What do the sales reps need to start or stop doing to more accurately submit deals to the pipeline?

1. _____

_____

2. _____

_____

3. _____

_____

Actions I need to take to change the team's behavior and obtain better forecasts:

1. _____

_____

2. _____

_____

3. _____

_____

 Impact of these changes for me, the team and organization:

1. _____

_____

2. _____

_____

3. _____

_____

Bonus Strategy! How will I keep both my changes and my team on track?

_____

_____

_____

_____

ANSWERS TO COMMON SALES ROADBLOCKS

"Sometimes the questions are complicated and the answers are simple."

Dr. Seuss

Create Sales Messages That Wow Prospects

"There's always room for a story that can transport people to another place." J.K. Rowling

Sales teams need descriptive and compelling sales messaging that help prospects connect with how your company and product benefits deliver real value. Developing and instructing your sales people on the Right messaging is critical to increased sales. So very often, sales people just can't figure out how to connect the dots between their company's benefits and features. As a result, they lack the confidence needed to sell up the chain into the C-Suite or to engage new contacts overall. I've heard from many a seasoned sales professional winding down on activity, "I just don't know what to say to stimulate interest once I get the meeting". Changes in company structure, vision and product line only exacerbate this.

Part of story telling's effectiveness lies in the universal themes that resonate with the listeners. It evokes a "Wow!" factor, nods of agreement, valuable insights and parallels that create thoughts like "that could happen to us!"

So take the time to develop compelling messaging that's weaved into your own story-- and make sure your sales team is well versed. Help them create a vivid picture in their own minds and for their customers of what you can provide. One that that they can clearly and repeatedly articulate.

Where are you going to take your prospects with <u>your</u> story? Here are 5 points to consider:

- What specific customer pains have you addressed that also relate to other prospects?

- What's a vision you want the prospect to imagine?

- What are the clear benefits other clients have gleaned from using your product and/ or service?

- What was the larger business impact of your solution on the prospects costs, sales or revenues?

- What made your offering uniquely qualified?

Consistent messaging among team members becomes a rallying cry . . . Get your team excited about their story and motivated to spread the good news. Customers and prospects benefit by getting a crystal clear vision of how your product or service provides distinct advantages to companies *just like theirs*. Make your story one of triumph over business challenges and a stimulus for growth!

"I'll Get Back to You"

Nothing's more frustrating to a salesperson than to have spent precious time with a hot prospect only to reach a dead end. You've covered all the bases only to get stuck sealing a deal due to lack of client commitment at the tail end. Need to create a sense of urgency to get your customer to order? Listen more . . . Talk less!

Respond to your customer's *"I'll think about it"* or *"I'll get back to you"* with open ended questions like these to uncover what the real issue is:

- *How do you evaluate a proposal like this?*

- *What could get in the way of moving forward?*

- *Who else needs to be involved?*

Be a good listener.   Restate their concerns with an *"I understand that [THEIR ISSUE]"*. Reframe their situation with how it plays into a need to act more sooner than later.

- Help the customer feel concern, doubt or uncertainties that could result from not acting now

- Ask *"What are the potential negative effects of waiting?"*, *"What is the cost [IN MONEY, TIME, QUALITY, QUANTITY] of a delay?"*

Review the financial and business benefits of acting without delay and tie these back to the customer's underlying business initiatives. Remind them of the pain that made them seek your solution in the first place. Ask questions that lead them to verbalize the value of your solution. Hearing themselves articulate it instead of you is forceful to their owning the desired results.

Create solid reasons for acting sooner rather than later. For example, use the time of year as in *"Upcoming summer vacations may require more lead time."* Or use potential events as in *"It's likely we may see price increases come January."*

Test different approaches and responses to see which ones get the best results.

Finally, reverse engineer what got you to this impasse in the first place and what you'll do differently the next time. Learn from the situation by:

- Validating your position well in advance of the close.

- Understanding your customer's interests, concerns and perceived risk in purchasing throughout the sales cycle.

- Reviewing each stage of the selling process from creating interest to close and analyzing which was not completed thoroughly.

- Making sure you and the customer have agreed on a timeline that is well documented.

- Being prepared for your "giveaways" and your "gets" in the negotiation process.

Align yourself with how your buyer buys by doing your homework, creating measurable value, accessing the true decision makers, controlling the process and developing the right competitive strategies. Proper execution throughout the Entire sales cycle ensures you negotiate a win-win close that puts you on the road to success --avoiding those paths that lead to nowhere.

Do You Have These Key Elements To Win The Deal?

Not every sales opportunity is going to be an ideal fit for your product, service or solution. To succeed in sales you need to know when to fish or cut bait! Top salespeople develop a keen sense of their situation and spend precious selling time on the deals with the highest probability of closing. They grasp whether the sale has potential for a timely win/win and allocate resources accordingly. When evaluating an existing or potential opportunity consider the following:

1. Where is the customer is in the buying cycle? Prospects must have business initiatives that create gaps and that require a fix that you can *jointly* solve to increase your odds of winning the sale. These latent pains are always the most deserving ones to pursue – those which you yourself can help a prospect identify and quantify. Most salespeople mistakenly seek out already live deals. But most often engagement for already active pains comes too late in the client's procurement process for you to successfully win. If they've already done their homework and have

begun shaping solutions by the time you've arrived you may be too late. Evaluate if you might end up spending a lot of cycles as column fodder in a bidding exercise for a solution that was co-created by a competitor.

2. Are you in contact with the right people? If you can't get direct access to decision makers, think again. Spending time with a prospect only to be denied a seat at the decision making table is foolhardy. Be sure early on that you have or can negotiate access to the people who actually commit funding and have signing authority. Don't fall prey to a scheme of having your contact doing your selling for you. Don't sell at your comfort level . . . Sell to the one making the decision.

3. Do you offer a differential advantage? If the client has commoditized the solution or your competitor clearly has an edge rethink strategy and further engagement. When vendor selection comes down strictly to price and the client sees no value in your offering it may be better to opt out early in the selling cycle – or spend as little resource and time as possible with the deal. Let your competitors play the price game and whittle their margins down to nothing in the process.

Understand clearly your product's sweet spot so you don't waste selling time with those who don't.

4. Are you in control of the sales process? If the prospect is getting from you without give on their part it may be time for you to move on. Engaging in opportunities where you can be proactive versus reactive greatly increases the odds of closing.

Your time is money and resources costly so be sure you put your energies into deals that can be positioned favorably and ultimately closed. Failing this, it may be best to exit and find another opportunity where you can play a central role in joint discovery of the client solution, create distinct value, connect with decision makers and manage the sales cycle.

Sadly, many salespeople are afraid of ticking their prospect off by being direct in their need for information and access. The goal is not to make your client like you – but respect you. Lack of confidence and respect may result in human nature taking over with buyers yanking you around to make sure their needs - not yours -are met. The goal is win/win . . .

How to Jumpstart A Stalled Sale

B2B salespeople have all experienced it. You've perfected the sales process by establishing value, credibility and trust. You and your customer come to clear agreement that the benefits of your offering solve his business challenges. But he just won't sign the order. In fact, he may even be as incommunicado as a shuttle astronaut on the other side of the moon. *"Houston, we have a problem."*

Even the most seasoned B2B salesperson has had a customer who just can't or won't order in spite of buying signals. Amazing though are the sales professionals who just wait . . . and wait . . . and wait. The more time that passes the more momentum you are losing. When a customer passes a deadline for action, contact them in one way shape or form the very next day. No reply? Don't let more than a couple of business days pass before reaching out yet again. Be **"professionally persistent"**.

To get your deal moving again be proactive with action orientated follow up and provide an impetus for ordering. What you don't want to do is react with desperation. A meteor shower of promotions (including price concessions!) is an invitation for the customer to wait even longer to see what else you can drum up as inducement. Instead, try these high impact ways to get the sales process unstuck:

- The vague *"I'm following up"* or *"checking in"* invites customer reply in alien-speak or no reply at all. Instead, be specific in your goal as in *"I am calling to learn the results of your meeting with finance."*

- When you aren't getting calls back mix it up with alternating or same day emails -- all with a strong call to action. Use attention grabbing email subject headers including key words such as "How to", "Discover", "Now" or "Why". Or use your cell phone which lacks your company's caller ID. Reaching out with both methods same day can also be effective. *"Per my email today . . ."* and *"Per my voicemail today . . ."* allow you to leverage both methods of communication professionally.

- Include Outlook email delivery receipt and read options. You'll get confirmation that your email isn't circling the stratosphere but has landed in an

Inbox and has been viewed which makes customers more likely to reply.

- Get face to face. Schedule a follow up meeting with an *"urgent update"* or with more *"information valuable to decision"* making for an opportunity to get to the bottom of the delay.

- Pretend to be an unintelligent life form. Ask the customer to help you understand the situation and tell them you are totally confused given your previous conversations. For most salespeople in limbo this isn't acting.

- Drill down past the icy layers in search of water and life. Respond to *"We're still deciding"* or *"We're not ready yet"* with specific questions: *"Where are you in the decision making process?"*, *"What obstacles are preventing you from moving forward with [THEIR BENEFIT]?"*, *"What has changed since we last talked?"*

- Develop a sense of urgency — i.e. the proposal pricing is expiring, its end of quarter and you need to prioritize back office workloads to meet delivery dates, etc.

- Follow up with a personal, handwritten note. Also consider sending via Fed Ex a personal follow up letter with a strong call to action to get the prospect's immediate attention.

Whatever methods you choose always be professional but most of all persistent. Don't assume you know why your customer isn't ordering. Many things could be getting in his the way like a genuine lack of time or manpower. So, don't keep circling out there in space. Go for the lunar landing and get those stalled B2B sales back on track.

TIPS FOR KEEPING YOUR PLAN ON TRACK

"Nothing in the world can take the place of persistence".

Calvin Coolidge

Find that you aren't achieving the goals you've established for yourself? Is your plan moving backwards, sideways or not at all? Don't let setbacks get you down. Instead, redouble your efforts or tweak your goal to get where you want or need to be. Stumbling blocks are going to be inevitable. They're a part of life! The trick is to be able to get back up on your horse.   The below questions will help you identify roadblocks, leverage strengths and get you back on the success track.

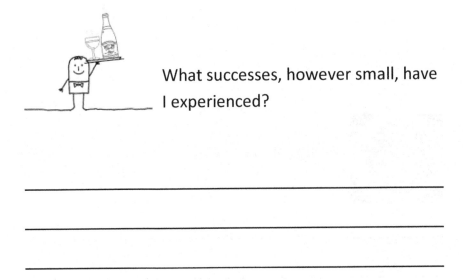 What successes, however small, have I experienced?

_____

_____

_____

What did I intend to complete but didn't?

_____

_____

_____

What got in the way?

_____

_____

_____

 Is the goal(s) still important to me and my sales career?

_____

_____

_____

 The benefits of successfully achieving my goal(s):

_____

_____

_____

_____

Three (3) things I can start doing to immediately to get me back on track:

1. _____

_____

2. _____

_____

3. _____

_____

Who can help me stay accountable for reaching my goal (family, friend, colleague, mentor, etc.)? How can they help me?

1. _____

_____

2. _____

   _____

3. _____

   _____

Bonus strategy! Brainstorm methods for remaining on task in the future.

_____

_____

Sadly, research shows[2] that there continues to be barriers to companies initiating in house sales coaching. Managers are too busy, they don't know when or who to coach, they're not accountable, they lack skills and coaching just isn't a priority for senior leadership so it doesn't get promoted. Truth is, sales people both want and need coaching. It's proven to be highly impactful and high performing organizations not coincidentally spend 15 to 20% more time coaching than lesser performing companies. The evidence shows that sales coaching is important but many companies simply fail to implement. Often the attitude is that coaching sales reps should fall under management "common sense" so it just never gets done or done properly.

Coaching is very much about self-awareness and making shift to achieve results. So congratulations on taking a step back to reflect and take charge of your own sales career! The coaching techniques in this little book pack much power for identifying and achieving your goals and are easily replicated for almost any career or personal situation. My aim is helping you discover a methodology for tackling problem sales situations time and time again . . . Happy selling!

---

[2] 2014 Sales Management Association, Obstacles to Coaching

SELLING RESOURCES & TOOLS

FREE Communications Assessment

The Talent Insights Report & Debrief

This comprehensive report reveals the **how**, **why and what** of individual performance. Identify, prioritize and calibrate sales or leadership performance criteria that will help you and your organization overcome today's challenges and increase sales.

To obtain your complimentary, custom report please email your request with "MY FREE ASSESSMENT" in the subject header to: AnnMarie@Parner4SuccessCoaching.com.

Offer subject to availability at time of request.

FREE Coaching Discovery Session

For more information on customized coaching and training programs for sales leaders, sales professionals or entire teams book a 50 minute consultation and laser coaching session.

 To schedule your complimentary session with me please email your request with "MY DISCOVERY SESSION" in the subject header to AnnMarie@Parner4SuccessCoaching.com.

Call Plan Template

Identify the prospect

Name:

_____

Business:

_____

Industry:

_____

Customers:

_____

Strategic partnerships:

_____

Corporate initiatives:

_____

Research the prospect

What specific business results do they need to achieve to accomplish the above initiatives (i.e. increase sales x%, enter markets, capture data, reduce expenses x%, upgrade business processes, improve financial results x%, etc.)?

_____

_____

_____

Look up recent press releases & weave the information into your customer conversations to demonstrate that you've done your homework and build credibility.

_____

_____

_____

What are their organizational issues and challenges stated in money, time, quality or quantity:

_____

_____

Are there any other internal or external compelling events (i.e. company reorganization, loss of a key customer, etc.)?

_____

_____

_____

What are the bigger industry trends and how is this customer affected?

_____

_____

_____

Who is their competition?

_____

_____

_____

What is their financial status, trends & recent results? Are there trends?

_____

_____

_____

Who is on the senior management team and what is their background? LinkedIn is a great source here!

_____

_____

_____

Create call objective

What is your call or meeting desired outcome: (Hint: The goal of your first/second face-to-face meeting should be discovery!).

_____

_____

_____

Determine collateral or presentation needed. Hint: Less is more!

_____

_____

_____

Made in the USA
Columbia, SC
06 February 2019